The B⌐
Britaɪ

by Ade Morris

SERVING THEATRE

S F

SINCE 1830

SAMUELFRENCH-LONDON.CO.UK
SAMUELFRENCH.COM

ISBN 978-0-573-11055-9

www.samuelfrench-london.co.uk

www.samuelfrench.com

FOR AMATEUR PRODUCTION ENQUIRIES

UNITED KINGDOM AND WORLD EXCLUDING NORTH AMERICA

plays@SamuelFrench-London.co.uk

020 7255 4302/01

UNITED STATES AND CANADA

info@SamuelFrench.com

1-866-598-8449

Each title is subject to availability from Samuel French, depending upon country of performance.

MUSIC USE NOTE

Licensees are solely responsible for obtaining formal written permission from copyright owners to use copyrighted music in the performance of this play and are strongly cautioned to do so. If no such permission is obtained by the licensee, then the licensee must use only original music that the licensee owns and controls. Licensees are solely responsible and liable for all music clearances and shall indemnify the copyright owners of the play(s) and their licensing agent, Samuel French, against any costs, expenses, losses and liabilities arising from the use of music by licensees. Please contact the appropriate music licensing authority in your territory for the rights to any incidental music.

IMPORTANT BILLING AND CREDIT REQUIREMENTS

If you have obtained performance rights to this title, please refer to your licensing agreement for important billing and credit requirements.

THE BOADICEA OF BRITANNIA STREET was first presented as *THE STORY OF A GREAT LADY* at The Watermill Theatre in Bagnor and on tour in Spring and Autumn 2007. The performance was directed by Ade Morris and designed by Libby Watson, with lighting by Lawrence T Doyle and original music by Paul Kissaun. The cast was as follows:

FRANCESCA LAMB . . . . Carrie Hinton

PENNY TEW . . . . Erica Rogers

ANNIE TAYLOR. . . . . Polly Highton

The play was much revised in this version, which was presented by Quidem Productions at the New Town Theatre at the Edinburgh Festival during August 2013. The performance was directed by Ade Morris and designed by Billy Smith, with lighting by Richard Bell and original music by Paul Kissaun. The cast was as follows:

FRANCESCA LAMB . . . . Lucinda Curtis

PENNY TEW . . . . Lizzie Lewis

ANNIE TAYLOR. . . . . Polly Highton

JANET MELLER. . . . . Alice Fyles

PERFORMANCE NOTES

The play is set in Winkham, a fictional small town somewhere in the North Midlands between Stoke-on-Trent and Manchester.

Most of the action is set on or in a backstage area of Winkham Memorial Institute. There are various bits of am-dram scenery, a props basket and a costume rail add functional clutter, amongst which is a useable 'prop' door in free-standing frame.

Stage right is a large props basket, stage left a piano under a dust sheet and a faded Union Jack flag. On top of the piano is a medium-sized round tea tin – which rattles.

There are four village hall-style plastic chairs, and an old table, much abused.

If set on a stage there could be a proscenium of sorts, perhaps faded curtains which can be opened and closed to top and tail Penny's narrative, an old backdrop revealed to indicate the view of Winkham, and a fore stage where the main action occurs...

Incidental music in the production was composed by Paul Kissaun as was music for the song *I'd Like To Be Like Boadicea*. Some of Paul's other atmospheric incidental music was based on the above song, while Paul's music linking most fast paced scenes was inspired by Benny Goodman's *Sing Sing Sing*. Use of the original incidental music is at the producer's discretion and all permissions can be obtained from Paul Kissaun, represented by T.C.G. Artist Management. The simple piano score for the 'Boadicea' song featured in the play is included in this edition.

Ade Morris

'I went to sea in a paper boat
to see if my paper boat would float...
It floated well
until a swell
drowned paper boat and me...
oh well'

In memory of the inspirational Jill Fraser, artistic director of the Watermill Theatre from 1981 - 2006

CHARACTERS

FRANCESCA LAMB – mid-60s, feisty, local journalist.

PENNY TEW – 30, shortish, a panicked P.E. teacher.

ANNIE TAYLOR – 40s, run to seed, plump, housewife.

JANET MELLER – 20s, librarian, shy, intense, repressed, reluctant pianist.

ACT ONE

Evening. Winkham Memorial Hall.

Music for opening, then underscore.

PENNY *speaks to the audience from stage right, a formal, slightly nervous manner.*

PENNY. For those of you who don't know me... I'm Penny. I first met Francesca, Fran, at the supermarket, Budgens.

FRAN *comes through the 'prop' door. She has a box of cat food. She peers into the darkness. She is at the back door of her house.*

She was trying to find pilchard cat snacks, I was trying to find baked beans... They'd moved everything around, you see, so there were all these women in there looking for things in all the wrong places – the story of my life...

FRANCESCA. SHAKESPEARE!!!

PENNY. Francesca's known to you all as editor of the arts page on the local paper, but she's also a published poet...

FRANCESCA. SHAKESPEARE! COME HERE YOU FLEA-INFESTED STINKER!!!

PENNY. ... really beautiful poetry actually...

FRAN *exits through the 'prop' door.*

(more relaxed by now) Anyway at this point I didn't know her, I was teaching P.E. at Winkham Comp, and I was a bit, well, frustrated... there's only so much you can do in P.E. at a comprehensive before you have to use guns and whips... Anyway on that last cross country race, half of Year Ten spent the afternoon in The Spotted

Dog and I was in the headmaster's office before you could say 'isotonic drinks'... So, during my second bottle of Côtes Du Rhône that night I read this ad in the *Winkham Weekly Snooze* and thought it was just the thing to take my mind off things... and I wasn't the only one. It was a wet night.

Huge clap of thunder and lightning, then torrential rain.

Bloody hell!... Very wet! And as I struggled down Britannia Street, Fran was already in the hall...

FRAN *is at Winkham Institute. She holds a bucket under the leaking roof.*

FRAN. *(talking to the empty hall as if to a packed meeting)* Thank you all so much for *not* coming along tonight, I must say I am *not* entirely chuffed by the turnout, I really had no idea that so many women in Winkham don't have even the slightest secret desire to be writers, so yes, I am a bit disappointed that you have *not* turned up, even in this bloody terrible weather, to try to touch once more, with me, the holy grail of creativity ... *(Another clap of thunder,* **FRAN** *reverts to normal)* All right keep your wig on!... I don't think we're going to experience anything holy tonight except the bloody roof – you miserable old Sod... *(She puts a bucket under a drip)*

PENNY *walks in, dripping wet.*

FRAN. *(to God)* I'm Sorry! *(to* **PENNY***)* Good evening!

PENNY. Hiya. Are you Francesca Lamb?

FRAN. Fran Lamb. It's less of a taradiddle.

PENNY. I saw the ad – the *Weekly Snooze?* This is the meeting, creative writing?

FRAN. Yes! – It started half an hour ago...

PENNY. Oh, sorry.

FRAN. Have you been swimming?

PENNY. No I walked, but it's chucking it down out there! Sorry, that's why I'm late.

FRAN. I'll find you a tea-towel or something.

PENNY.Don't worry, soaking'll do me good, I might grow a bit – like a pot plant

FRAN. Well sit by the radiator, we can watch you steam, want a cup of tea?

PENNY. Love one... Gasping.

> FRAN *starts to make tea.*

> Milk, four sugars thanks... So, how many are you expecting?

FRAN. You're it so far.

PENNY. What do you mean?

FRAN. On your shoulders rests all hope for the literary life of Winkham. I hope you can write?

PENNY. I've never really tried. Well, a bit, but you know...

FRAN. Then hope sinks, like a legless frog, into the pond of oblivion...

PENNY. Sorry...?

FRAN. Only joking, dear.

PENNY. There'll be more, I'm sure, we just have to wait... perhaps... they're in the toilet.

FRAN. Heavens! Another optimist, I thought we were all dead?

PENNY. I try to look on the bright side.

FRAN. Me too. Me too...*(she waves the vodka)* Liquid inspiration?

PENNY. Can you have vodka in tea?

FRAN. You can have vodka in anything, dear...

> FRAN *gets a green cup from the institute cupboard and pours a tot into* PENNY*'s tea.*

> So, what's your name?

PENNY. Penny. Penny Tew.

FRAN. Who the hell called you that?

PENNY. My dad thought it was funny. My mum divorced him, when I was a kid.

FRAN. Do you see him still?

PENNY. He remarried. He sends Christmas cards, you know...

FRAN. And your mum?

PENNY. Oh I still live with her. She works at Wilko's.

FRAN. She marry again?

PENNY. She'd be lucky. This twenty questions?

FRAN. I'm interested, it's my job.

PENNY. She's tricky, my mum, always has been. She likes a drink.

FRAN. Don't we all?

PENNY. I try not to, drink. I mean usually... I think there might be a family weakness, you know, sherry soaked afternoons watching *Bargain Hunt*...

Beat. Suddenly FRAN *recognises* PENNY.

FRAN. Budgens!

PENNY. Well yeah, they do have quite a nice cheap sherry.

FRAN. No! That's where I've seen you before, been wondering—

PENNY. Pilchard cat snacks!

FRAN. Baked beans!

PENNY. Yes that's it, that's what they call me... Miss Baked Bean.

Pause.

FRAN. So, you're a teacher.

PENNY. How can you tell?

FRAN. Fear of alcoholism, sensible shoes and a nervous twitch...

PENNY. P.E. teacher, Winkham Comp.

FRAN. P.E.? I thought P.E. teachers were all shrink-wrapped in Lycra?

PENNY. Not really, teaching P.E. is a form of self-harm for people who can't teach...

FRAN. So what brings you here?

PENNY. Oh you know, need to do something to take my mind off something else, that sort of thing...

FRAN. Going to tell me what sort of thing?

PENNY. Not yet, no.

Pause. They drink their tea.

What about you? Life in a nutshell?

FRAN. OK. Fran Lamb. Francesca only to my mother, now deceased, old age. Dad died in a tank in Korea. Happyish childhood with Mum despite that, happy adulthood, with Harry, my other half, he died last year, pretty upset about that... No children. Work for the *Winkham Weekly Snooze*, coming up to retirement, can't think where the last forty years went!

PENNY. I'm sorry.

FRAN. Oh don't be, wouldn't change a thing.

PENNY. No, I mean sorry about your husband dying...and everyone else.

FRAN. Oh... Yes... Thank you. These things happen...

PENNY. You were close...

FRAN. Yes we were... Very... got a vicious old Tom bastard of a cat now... and I was standing at the back door the other night and I just thought, this is it. I'm an old woman standing at her back door calling a bloody cat, like all the other old fleabags...

PENNY. Cats?

FRAN. Old women. The brittle backbones of England. I'm too young to be old. I'm only sixty-four, that's not really old is it?

PENNY. No, that's not old...

FRAN. How old is your difficult mum that you can't stand?

PENNY. Sixty-four.

A clap of thunder.

ANNIE *enters through the 'prop' door, a plump middle-aged woman in a black balaclava helmet and carrying* *a golf umbrella. She is followed by* **JANET**, *a shy-looking girl in a Millets mac.*

ANNIE. Is this the Winkham Women Writers Troop?

FRAN. No, this is Winkham Alcoholics Anonymous. Who are you? Have the council sent a hit man?

ANNIE *takes off her balaclava.*

ANNIE. Stop mucking about, I'm dropping wet!

FRAN. Where did you get that balaclava from?

ANNIE. Army surplus. Keith says it hides my feminosity, like a Yashmick.

PENNY. Yashmak?

FRAN. Are you a dyslexic, dear?

ANNIE. No, I'm a housewife, but I want to learn how to write literally. So does she, her name's Janet, isn't it, love?

JANET *nods, shyly.*

Are we in the right place?

FRAN. I'm not sure, dear… Why do you need to disguise your feminosity?

ANNIE. Keith say's it'll put off other men.

FRAN. This is the Winkham Memorial Institute dear, it is a sex exclusion zone.

ANNIE. You hear that, Janet? You're out of luck!

PENNY. It might actually attract other men, the Yashmak.

ANNIE. Balaclava. How?

PENNY. Well they might think you had something to hide.

ANNIE. What exactly are you saying?

PENNY. Oh, pants! I'm sorry, no that's not what I meant… I mean you do have something to hide, plenty to hide… Oh God!

ANNIE. You'd better watch it, you… digit.

FRAN. Midget.

PENNY. I'm nearly as tall as you!

ANNIE. Not horizontally!

FRAN. Now, now, ladies, this is a community of creativity we're trying to form... Let's all calm down and be friends, shall we? Shall we? Janet, tell us all about yourself.

JANET. My name's Janet.

FRAN. Yes I think we've gleaned that dear. You look familiar, are you a Budgens shopper too?

JANET. The library. I work in the library. Er, I'm a librarian.

FRAN. Of course you are! Isn't she?

They silently agree.

FRAN. I'm Fran Lamb. *(she holds out both hands.)*

Both shake.

This is Penny, she's an alcoholic.

PENNY. I am not an alcoholic! My mother's an alcoholic, I'm just dribbling... Dabbling! *(also shaking ANNIE's and JANET's hands)*

ANNIE. Annie Taylor, squeezed to meet you both, so's Janet, aren't you, Janet?

JANET. Yes.

FRAN. We should get started... A few moments ago I was alone, and now I have three companions in search of the spirit of the poets – together we will tread the twinkling firmament of creation!

JANET. Great

ANNIE. Scooper

PENNY. Anyone fancy another cuppa, it's just boiled?

ANNIE. Smashin'.

FRAN. Help yourself to more booze...

JANET. I don't really like it, sorry.

FRAN. What's the matter with young people today?

ANNIE. I'm not young. I'll have some.

PENNY. Me too!

FRAN. You're younger than me dear, age is in the eyes of the mirror. We should get started... Look lets all sit down and think about what to do next.

PENNY. How exciting...

ANNIE. Before we actually start, I think I should say, I mean, I have to say, that I've never written a turd in my life, you know, a creative turd.

JANET. Word?

PENNY. Are you her translator or summat?

JANET. Er, no I'm just try—

PENNY. Is this a weird form of Tourette's you have?

ANNIE. It's my swerves.

JANET. Nerves.

ANNIE. Yes! When I get the swerves there's a bad connection in my pain.

PENNY. Oh God...

FRAN. Well that's never held back some of our most famous writers, dear...

ANNIE. Hasn't it?

FRAN. Lack of coherence is the least of your problems when it comes to writing...

JANET. Really?

FRAN. When I was a young writer on the paper – I thought, what on earth do I write about? I didn't have a story in me, not a sausage, and then the most magnificent thing happened... A life-changing moment!

ANNIE. Insulation?

JANET. Inspiration!

FRAN. Deadlines. Somebody died, then somebody else... and the bloody paper still needed writing.

ANNIE. Lucky.

PENNY. Not for the dead ones...

FRAN. I started as a reviewer... obituaries as well, which were often pretty similar...

JANET. And poems...

ANNIE. Poems?

FRAN. One or two... Now, Annie, coherence is a complete disadvantage when it comes to poetry...

JANET. You've written loads of poems. I've read your collection, *Paper Boats*, I loved it! That's why I'm here.

JANET *quotes, suddenly intense.*

'I WENT TO SEA IN MY PAPER BOAT
TO SEE IF MY PAPER BOAT WOULD FLOAT...
IT FLOATED WELL
UNTIL A SWELL
DROWNED PAPER BOAT
AND ME
(OH WELL)...

FRAN. And etceteraa... etceteraaa!... It was you that bought it then... I often wondered... You can stay, you lovely girl...

ANNIE. And me?

FRAN. We are here to free your creativity like a lusty mare in search of a wild stallion!

ANNIE. Are we...!?

FRAN. And I will be handing out the deadlines myself!

ANNIE. Deadlines?

FRAN. That magificent word. 'A deadline means that words must appear on paper...' Repeat with me.

ALL. 'A deadline means that words (ANNIE *says 'turds')* must appear on paper.'

FRAN. So, by the time we three meet again I want you all to have thought of... Well, a poem... Why not!... To read aloud to the group, it needn't be any good...

ANNIE. What about?

FRAN. Anything you like, having a poo for all I care, and Penny..

PENNY. Yes...

FRAN. As you're a P.E. teacher I'd like you to start us all off next week with a nice little exercise, something to get our minds and bodies ticking over like well-oiled machines.

ANNIE. I'm not sure my body will do flipping over like a well oiled machine.

PENNY. I'm not that sort of P .E. teacher!

FRAN. Really?

PENNY. I'm cerebral, I do theory...

FRAN. Oh.

PENNY. ... I don't actually like P.E., as such, I just like the idea of it.

FRAN. Why are you teaching it then?

PENNY. My Dad was a P .E. teacher, it's genetic, like a disease...

FRAN. Well could you do a cerebral warm up? Exercise for the mind, we don't have to actually move?

ANNIE. Sounds more like it...

PENNY. Anyway I thought this was supposed to be about learning how to write, ... not just being told to go away and do it, that's what I do at school.

FRAN. Ah but that's the key to it. Very rarely does anybody write anything because it pops into their head. There has to be a reason, some cause... War, poverty and bad sex have inspired more great writers than you could count.

ANNIE. I don't think Winkham's big on war and novelty. Bad sex might be a possibility...

PENNY. I know all about bad sex, I could write the Rough Guide!

JANET. If you write it, can I read it?

FRAN. Writing is all about living, about letting life burn your wings. You can't do it unless – unless dreadful and brilliant things happen to you.

JANET. You talk like a poet. You're all... inflammable.

FRAN. So next week, when we four meet again, we will all be dreadful – and – we will all be brilliant!

PENNY. Or brilliantly dreadful?

JANET. Or dreadfully brilliant!

FRAN. You're getting the idea!

Music, then dipping to underscore.

PENNY *is alone again. As she speaks, the scene changes.*

PENNY. So over the next week I tried to put something on paper, and believe me it wasn't easy, I mean I know my work's supposed to be a bit creative, but teaching for me was all about screaming at teenagers the size of gorillas, with the intellect of fish and the sex drive of rabbits. I felt about as creative as a used condom.

Back with FRAN, JANET *and* ANNIE, *the following week.*

FRAN. Right Penny, what have you got for us? I want to feel the blood in my veins... Your warm up?

PENNY. A warm up? You still serious?

FRAN. Never more so!

ANNIE. I'm not cold, I've got my squermals on.

FRAN. That's not the point Annie, and you're far too young for thermals.

ANNIE. Is there an age when you're old enough?

FRAN. Around 48/49 - depending on your circulation - or your sex life.

ANNIE. Well I've got blood like iced Ribena.

FRAN. Then you need it boiling up! – Penny?

ANNIE. Anyway I thought this was creative writing, not weight watchers...

FRAN. Creative writing is slimming for the mind, a lean, hard brain is the aim... Penny?

PENNY. I don't do this sort of thing anymore, it's too dangerous, there are health and safety considerations.

FRAN. We are not teenagers, or even young, at least I am not. You are safe from the cruel scent of testosterone or Biactol... Come on!

PENNY. Er... Well there's something I used to do... at training college... You all need to stand up.

FRAN, JANET *and* PENNY *stand up.*

ANNIE. I'm not standing up.

PENNY. No, of course not, sorry.

FRAN. Why not?

ANNIE. Because I'm not, I don't like this sort of thing.

FRAN. What sort of thing?

ANNIE. All this modern stuff, exercise. Anyway I thought we'd come here to learn how to write?

FRAN. It's to get us all in the mood, loosened up

ANNIE. I don't want loosening up, I like being tight!

PENNY. I would not describe you as tight.

FRAN. This is different...

JANET. Come on Annie, it won't hurt...

FRAN. Well it might a bit, but it' s good pain.

> ANNIE *still does not stand up.*

ANNIE. If I stand up. I'm not taking my shoes and socks off.

PENNY. Did I ask you to take your shoes and socks off?

ANNIE. No... but you might.

PENNY. I have no interest in your feet! Why would I want you to take your shoes and socks off!

ANNIE. I did one of these warm up flings before, they made us all take our shoes and socks off...

PENNY. When was this?

ANNIE. When I was six, at school. I've never begotten it.

PENNY. Scarred for life were you?

ANNIE. Too right! The whole class was. It was a vilification of our basic human tights.

PENNY. OK! So I won't ask you to take your socks off but please, please stand up! *(teacher voice)* ANNIE TAYLOR NOW!

ANNIE. Oh God! *(she stands up)*

PENNY. This is worse than Winkham Comp! Now, just, loosen up a little, raise one shoulder...then the other... *(FRAN is fine, very subtle, ANNIE ends up with both shoulders raised)* Then shake one hand like this... then shake the other... *(ANNIE alone keeps shaking the hand that was shaking before)* that's it... Now spread your legs...

ANNIE. I'm not spreading my legs!

JANET. How far? *(almost, or actually if possible, doing the splits)*

PENNY. That's enough! Now slowly bend over and touch the floor, ligament by ligament *(ANNIE keels over, hands on the floor with a thump, bum in the air)* And now lets slowly go up again, joint by joint. *(ANNIE tries, but fails, with a few grunts)*

ANNIE. I'm bloody stuck!!!

FRAN. Better help her...

ANNIE. I told you! I'm not built for bending.

FRAN. You'd better lie down, you too Penny, Janet.

PENNY. Are we doing writing now?

FRAN. Yes Penny we're doing writing, or something on the way to writing, come on, lie down

ANNIE. Do we have to write lying down!?

FRAN. We're going to stimulate our imaginations.

ANNIE. Is that legal on council property?

JANET. Come on Annie...

> **PENNY** *and* **ANNIE** *lie down.*

FRAN. It won't hurt for a minute!

ANNIE. The floor's cold and sticky...

PENNY. This is why I can't do this! Now you know what it's like in comprehensive education.

FRAN. Please Annie?... Annie?

> *Beat.*

ANNIE. I'm all ears! *(She lies down)*

FRAN. Right. I want you to close your eyes, relax, breathe deeply, and imagine... Imagine that you're not cold and sticky. Imagine that you're on a desert island, the sun is warming your whole body, there are exotic birds in the high palms all around you, and in front of you is a wide, white, sandy beach, turquoise sea lapping on the shore... Now lets make some of these sounds, lets make this seem real...

FRAN *begins to make a swishing sound, then* JANET *joins in with a very loud and harsh parrot.*

ANNIE. Can I rent a deck chair?

FRAN. Right that's enough noise, it's a silent island now... And in the distance, sailing toward you, a tall – masted Galleon, a solitary figure on the prow whose silhouette you recognise from a dream. Just watch the ship for a little while... See the sea break at the bow.... and listen to the peace of the sea on your beach, everywhere the lapping of the waves, the approaching ship, with the mysterious figure, listen to the sea... Now... When you know, when you're certain... can you tell me who is coming towards you on that distant ship?

ANNIE. I need the toilet!

FRAN. Annie!

ANNIE. It's all this lapping water !

FRAN. You're supposed to be in the moment, lose control!

ANNIE. If I lose control now you'll regret it!

FRAN. Oh go on then.

ANNIE. Thanks Miss...

ANNIE *scuttles out, a slience falls.*

JANET. It was kate Winslet.

FRAN. What was?

JANET. Coming towards me on that boat, like in 'Titanic'.

FRAN. Good. Well I'm glad it rang your bell Janet... Penny? *(then there is a gentle snoring)* Penny? ... Penny...

PENNY *is asleep.*

FRAN. Oh for God's sake!

Music. Later that same evening, FRAN, JANET AND ANNIE *are having a cup of tea on the forestage.* PENNY *joins them.*

PENNY. So how long was I asleep for?

PENNY. Forty-five minutes, we had a lovely cup of tea didn't we?

JANET. Well it was all right...

ANNIE. There were no biscuits.

PENNY. You should have woken me up.

ANNIE. It seemed a shame to, you were snoring like a pooper.

JANET. Trooper.

PENNY. I've been really tired lately... you have to get up at the crap of dawn to get to school.

ANNIE. I could do with being tired, I never sleep a blink.

JANET. Wink.

ANNIE. Why?

JANET. You never sleep a wink.

ANNIE. That's what I said... What?

JANET. Oh never mind...

FRAN. Anyway now we're all awake again, last week I set you some homework, how did you get on?

ANNIE. Not... brolliant.

PENNY. I'll second that, not brolliant at all!

FRAN. It doesn't have to be 'brolliant!'... Annie, did you write anything creative?

ANNIE. Well yes, and, no.

FRAN. Which?

ANNIE. No. I didn't actually write anything... But yes I did... create something.

FRAN. Please go on.

ANNIE. It's a twist, of things, sort've collected.

FRAN. A list? Sounds very promising, will you read it.

ANNIE. It's all rubbish.

FRAN. I said it doesn't need to be good.

ANNIE. No it is all rubbish, actual rubbish... it's a twist of rubbish, stuff that went in the bin this morning.

FRAN. Read it please.

> ANNIE *composes herself, very nervous. She takes a piece of paper from her pocket, itsef the back of an old envelope.*

ANNIE. Don't say I didn't horn you duck...

JANET. Warn... Sorry

> **ANNIE** *clears her throat and etc., at some length, then begins.*

ANNIE. Teabag, PG tits Tin which held Chum Tissue with which I wiped dog's... nose.

> *(to* **PENNY** *and* **FRAN**) Bum would've rhymed I know, but it wasn't true...

FRAN. Beauty is truth, truth beauty, please go on...

ANNIE. Double glazing offer from a company in Surrey, empty Cornflake racket full of last night's slurry.

JANET. Curry?

ANNIE. Slurry, yes *(to* **PENNY** *and* **FRAN**) Well I had to put it somewhere, and if you put it straight in the bin it seeps out of the bin's bottom days later...

'Screw Fix' catalogue
Other mail that's come...
No one writes proper letters anymore
Not like my Mum..... used to

PENNY. That's true that...

ANNIE. *Pair of old pants,*
Holes in front and rear
Jar of Budgens own-brand jam
...Expired last year

(to **PENNY, JANET** *and* **FRAN**) Do you want some more, I told you it was all rubbish?

FRAN. Is there more?

ANNIE. Oh yes.

FRAN. Then I can hardly wait...

ANNIE. *Another teabag, empty biscuit slapper.*

(to **PENNY, JANET** *and* **FRAN**) This was a bit later, like...

> *Crusty, ripped bag of sugar.*
>
> *(to* **PENNY, JANET** *and* **FRAN**) You know, with all brown round the top where the spoons gone in.

FRAN. Absolutely...

ANNIE. *ripped bag of sugar... 36 of Keith's fag ends.*
'Cus he' s a lazy sodding... (a struggle) bugger! (*to* PENNY,
JANET *and* FRAN) ... That last bit is about Keith, my
husband, he is a lazy slugger... I'd not say it to his face,
but it's quite nice I can say it here, like... Keith. Is a lazy
sodding slugger!

FRAN. And that takes you how far into your day?

ANNIE. About 11.30, it's a work in progress...

JANET. I quite liked it...

PENNY. Me too.

FRAN. So did I, it showed enormous promise and originality.

ANNIE. You're taking the pish.

JANET/PENNY/FRAN. No we're not!

FRAN. No we're not. I think it comes from life, I was
intrigued by the damning reference to Keith, tell us
about Keith.

ANNIE. What's to tell?

FRAN. Well I don't know, he's not my husband...

ANNIE. Well. He'd kill me if he knew I was near.

JANET. Here?

FRAN. Really? Why?

ANNIE. He thinks I've gone to see my brother, she's up at
the hotspot.

PENNY. Your brother's a girl?

ANNIE. Brother! You know, gave birth to me!

JANET. Ah… Mother…

ANNIE. Anyway, Keith, he's always been against the farts...

JANET. Arts?

ANNIE. That's what I said. Keith says it rots the mind, he
says it's where my mother went wrong. That's why she's
at the hotspot, you know, on the mount...

JANET. Ah! Hospice.

ANNIE. She doesn't know what she means anymore, they
say she's fermented.

JANET. Demented.

PENNY. Really?

ANNIE. She's much worse than me...

FRAN. Oh dear.

ANNIE. So I go up there, and I listen. It's a bit sad, I feel sad listening to her. And that's why I thought this might be good, like, I don't want to end up like that...

FRAN. She was creative?

ANNIE. She was in Winkham Amateur Dramatic Society for thirty-five years.

FRAN. That reminds me, they're organising a festival, it's all about trying to find promising new writers.

PENNY. So?

FRAN. So I thought we could enter it, with a new play... or whatever.

PENNY. What new play?

FRAN. Well it doesn't have to be a play, it could be lots of bits – but it needs to be performable.

PENNY. Performable!

ANNIE. I've always wanted to write a play.

PENNY. Now she thinks she's Dawn French.

FRAN. Let's hear yours then?

PENNY. Eh?

FRAN. Your writing? You haven't read anything out yet.

PENNY. Well... I don't think it's any good.

FRAN. Annie's had her turn, now you have to do yours, and then we'll have Janet's.

JANET. Mine's more of an idea...

FRAN. Whatever, ideas are good, Penny, come along now.

PENNY *takes out a sheet of folded paper.*

PENNY. All right! I'm not saying I'm not going to do it am I? I'm just a bit embarrassed, I thought these creative writing things are supposed to be no pressure and no putting people on the spit... spot!

FRAN. Not on my time they're not... pressure and pain help spill the visceral juice of creation... so your thing, please.

PENNY. Look, it's a bit personal.

FRAN. Would you like to stand on the table and take your clothes off?

PENNY. No I would not like to stand on the table and take my bloody clothes off!

FRAN. Then think how much easier and less embarrassing it's going to be to just read it...

A pause. PENNY *unfolds the paper, then tentatively reads.*

PENNY.
ALONE
A SINGLE TREE
NO ONE TO HELP ME STAND
ALONE
A FLY IN THE OINTMENT
A WASP IN A JAR
A TEAR IN THE EYE
OF A CHEESY PRINT
ALONE
A COLD FIRE
A BLUNTED FLINT.

A silence. They are slightly taken aback, then ANNIE *starts clapping.*

ANNIE. That was bountiful!!! Really bountiful!!!

FRAN. It is very 'bountiful', well done, Penny.

JANET. I thought you said you can't write?

PENNY. I can't, that's just what goes through my head all day, the same self-pitying dirge, it's depressing.

ANNIE. Well I can pee that, duck.

FRAN. No boyfriend then?

ANNIE. Ahhhh...

PENNY. I have trouble with men, the last one called me his little dwarf.

FRAN. You're too tall to be a dwarf, and anyway even if you were you're a very attractive dwarf. Isn't she Janet? Are you allowed to say dwarf anymore? I never know about these things 'till I put my foot in it?

PENNY. No you're not, not in schools anyway.

ANNIE. Dwarf is quite a nice turd... It's in Disney.

JANET. I suppose you can't say it in case you happen to be standing next to a dwarf...

ANNIE. What if you're Snow White?

JANET. Well if you're Snow White that's different, you'd expect to be standing next to a dwarf, in fact several dwarfs.

FRAN. Seven dwarfs.

JANET: Yes. If you were Snow White.

ANNIE. It's digits you can't say, but you are much bigger than a digit, you're just skinny.

PENNY. Skinny midget. Thanks very much, my self esteem is really boosted.

ANNIE. You should put an ad in the paper if you want a toyfriend, that way he won't know you're a digit 'til he meets you.

PENNY. I'm not a midget! I'm just short! And I don't want a 'toyfriend', I never want a bloody toyfriend in my life again – OK?!!

ANNIE. Fine! Keep your chair on...! *(to the others)* Touched a swerve there then.

PENNY. You have not touched a 'swerve'! My interest in men is a thing of the past, for personal and private reasons!!!

Pause. They all look at **PENNY.** **FRAN** *starts again.*

FRAN. Anyway, this festival—

ANNIE. I'm not sure I'm up to a bestival.

FRAN. It's all for charity so what harm can it do?

PENNY. Which charity?

FRAN. Cancer, I think.

ANNIE. My mother's got that as well.

FRAN. I'm sorry.

ANNIE. Oh don't be, she's had them all, she's like a terminus, the Crewe Station of cancer, but she's fine, it's the fermentia that's the problem...

FRAN. Yes, poor lady.

ANNIE. She has weed.

PENNY. Incontinence as well?

ANNIE. No! Weeeeed. The drug. She smokes it on description for the rain.

JANET. Pain?

ANNIE. Yes. Now they can't get her off it, the care home smells like Winkham bus station on a Friday tight...

FRAN. That's fantastic, we could put her in the play, or whatever it is...

PENNY. What are we going to write a play, or whatever it is, about?

JANET. Women!

All look at JANET.

PENNY. Women?

FRAN. Janet, is this your big idea?

JANET. Yes. Women in England, but I don't know how to write a play.

FRAN. – Maybe they could all be seen through the prism of one particular woman's experiences?

JANET. Someone ancient, legendary...

ANNIE. Madonna?

PENNY. Barbara Windsor?

FRAN. How about... Boadicea?

ANNIE. What?

JANET. Yes! Perfect!

FRAN. Great minds think alike Janet!

ANNIE. Who is she?

FRAN. Ancient British East Anglian Queen

ANNIE/PENNY. Why?

FRAN. Because the Romans stole her land and raped her daughters, and she was very, very, annoyed.

ANNIE. No I mean why do you want us to write a play about an East Anglican?

JANET. Anglian.

FRAN. Well, Annie, you could say why write a play about anything, couldn't you? Because she's there?... Janet?

JANET. Maybe to find her historical presence in the make-up of the modern woman!

ANNIE. I can't wear make-up, I've got sensitive sin.

PENNY. 'Boudicca'.

FRAN. What?

PENNY. 'Boudicca', that's what they call her now.

FRAN/ANNIE. Who?

PENNY. In school, you know, that's how it's written in all the books now, 'Boudicca', we did a project...

FRAN. Well I'd rather call her Boadicea, no one over fifty's going to know who the hell 'Boudicca' is are they?

ANNIE. Yeah but why do you want us to write a play?

PENNY. Or whatever it is...

ANNIE. About Bowd— about Bood— about this Anglican?

FRAN. She could be a way of examining our own identities without going up our own bottoms, couldn't she, Janet?

JANET. Definitely.

ANNIE. Why would I want to go up my own bottom?

PENNY. Anyway this is a bit of a leap isn't it, from two rubbish poems to Queen Boadacea's bottom?

FRAN. They're not rubbish poems, if they were bad I'd say, but they just aren't. And the reason they're not is that you both laid bare the ample bosoms of your souls, like naked ladies on a beach washed by the cleansing tide of truth... and then along comes the shipwrecked sex-starved sailor of Janet's big idea!

PENNY. Your mind is weird...

ANNIE. I wrote about rubbish, I never mentioned ample cousins!

FRAN. Bosoms! Do you want me to tell you what that says about your life... that you wrote about rubbish?

PENNY. Here we go...

FRAN. What do you mean 'here we go'.

PENNY. I don't need a psychiatrist, I just want to express myself!

FRAN. But that's what it's all about! It's like turning on the runway lights in your head... So big fat ideas can land at the Manchester Airport of your mind like... like flying hippoptamuses... Take your poem Penny, how did you feel when you'd read it?

PENNY. Relieved, probably like I would if a flying hippopatamus landed safely at Manchester.

FRAN. Just because you'd read it?

PENNY. Yeah...

FRAN. And anything else?

PENNY. Well because I'd told you something I suppose, that I wanted you to know.

FRAN. That you're a bit lonely sometimes?

PENNY. Yes... So, what about it?

FRAN. And does that mean you need a psychiatrist?

PENNY. Well of course not, no...But a friend might be nice.

FRAN. Rich, devoted, good in bed?

PENNY: Well I was thinking of someone just to talk to for starters, but one thing might lead to another...

FRAN. Precisely! Exactly! I think if we write something about a woman we've never met, then we'll find out all sorts of things about each other, and then we'll find her, this extraordinary woman from history.

PENNY. What will we do with her if we find her?

FRAN. We'll listen to what she says.

PENNY. You talk as if she's going to just walk in here with a shield and a sword.

FRAN. She might, next week she might... I want you to find out about her, and report back here...

PENNY. How?

FRAN. Read a book or something.

PENNY. Read a book! I'm a teacher! I haven't got time to read a book!

FRAN. Well try the Internet, then... or go to Janet's library before they close it.

ANNIE. My Keith won't let me near the interweb, says it's full of pornographs and paedoflies.

FRAN. I just want you back here next week – like eager young ferrets from up the dark trouser leg of history...

ANNIE. Ferrets?...

FRAN. Furry things with teeth, Annie. It's a metaphor. A thing that stands for something else.

ANNIE. Like a stick holding up a plant?

FRAN. No. That is just a stick holding up a plant.

ANNIE. That's what I want to blow, you see – how to write.

PENNY. You can barely speak!

ANNIE. You starting again, you nasty little... sprogget?

PENNY. Go eat a doughnut!

FRAN. We could make up a song, or the start of a song, shall we?

JANET. Yes please!

FRAN. I can't really sing, but I can make up some words... and a bit of a tune...

IF BOADICEA
WAS HERE TODAY
WOULD SHE FIGHT ROMANS
SCARE THEM AWAY?
...how's that...?

JANET. It's fab!

FRAN. Can you play the piano?

JANET. I can play with one finger. But not since I've grown up.

FRAN. Then be a girl again! Come and play it now.

JANET. What, right now?

FRAN. Yes, go on! *(clearing the dust-cloths from the piano)* Something all diddly doo...

ANNIE. I've got an instrument.

FRAN. Good, good! Come on, Janet, we can record it on this so we don't forget. *(producing a Dictaphone)*

JANET. It'll be terrible...

FRAN. Never mind, go on!

(*JANET starts to play a halting tune on the piano, trying to find the melody.*)

That's quite good, so that would go... (*JANET and FRAN sing to the tune.*)

IF BOADICEA
WAS HERE TODAY
WOULD SHE FIGHT ROMANS
SCARE THEM AWAY?

WOULD SHE BE BRAVE
AND WOULD SHE BE BOLD
LIKE A WOMAN WITH STRENGTH
LIKE A WOMAN OF OLD?

Yes, yes! Janet, you can write some more words! We need a chorus! Annie, bring your instrument next week, what is it? Guitar? Recorder?

PENNY. Tuba? Steel drums? Bag pipes?

ANNIE. Yeah... Something like that.

Music as the scene changes, to underscore for Penny.

ANNIE and **FRAN** exit upstage. **JANET** remains at the piano.

PENNY. *(to audience)* So there I was with Janet in Winkham library, trying to find out about a dead British queen called Boadicea, and you know what, there's not a lot to find. Once you've got the basics: father died, she inherits the kingdom, Romans want it, she's pretty good at killing Romans – who either killed her and all her friends and relations straight back – or she topped herself with poison, probably buried under a Burger King in Bromsgove... anyway, I printed some stuff off.

Another meeting. **ANNIE** *is not there yet.*

FRAN *returns and is in mid-conversation with* **PENNY**. **JANET** *is practising on the piano...*

FRAN. Well precisely, that's why she's such a good subject, we can turn her into whoever we want her to be...

PENNY. That doesn't seem right, you know, like lying.

FRAN. All the best writers are pathological liars!

JANET. Are they?

FRAN. Yes! What's the most borrowed category of books in your library, Janet?

JANET. Fiction, usually romantic, with lots of sex...

FRAN. And is your life like that?

JANET. I wish it was...

FRAN. So why fiction? Because the truth is so painful! Imagine you're a writer stuck in the corner of some rented room, with nothing but an economy light bulb, damp ginger nuts, and a blank sheet of paper, so you start to live in a fantasy world... If you want wings, then you can write them in, stick them on your back with Sellotape and fly over Winkham singing *(she leaps onto a chair) Jesus Christ Superstar!*... It's all in your head... Oh dear.

She sits, seems suddenly very tired.

PENNY. Are you all right?

FRAN. *(pulling herself together)* I'm fine... so we've got the basics, but what do we really know about Boadicea then? The person she was?

JANET. Shouldn't we wait for Annie?

FRAN. She can join in when she gets here. Boadicea? Let's write a speech about how she feels at the start...

PENNY. What, just like that?

FRAN. Yes! The scenario is the bones, now we need the flesh... As the writer you have to get inside the characters, you have to feel it and as you feel it you might find out what it's all about, the sub-text as they say, you know, besides just being about Boadicea in a field outside Bromsgrove.

PENNY. Sorry I...

FRAN. The Scenario's just the coat hanger, the play is the frock! It's like the boat thing, who's on the boat, who's coming over the sea?

PENNY. I was asleep when you did that.

FRAN: Yes I know! So, come on, you've just heard of your father's death, you're wondering if you can cut the mustard as queen of the Iceni, you're staring at the grey and threatening sea, what are you thinking? Come on, you're a teacher, improvise.

PENNY. Fran, I—

FRAN. Janet can do the sound effects, the swishing sea sort've thing!

JANET. Oo good, I'll use this bottle of water!

PENNY. I'm not sure that'll help...

FRAN. What's the matter with you, where's your confidence?

PENNY. Well that's the whole point! I've had the confidence sucked out of me by vampire teenagers!

FRAN. Rubbish! Just do it! Janet, the sea, the sea... Get up on the chair, Penny, be tall, powerful!

JANET *starts doing the sound effects with a bottle of Budgens mineral water.*

PENNY. Oh God... Er... I am a queen now...

FRAN. Good...

PENNY. But will I be a queen forever?

FRAN. Self-doubt, very good, really become the character, let her fill your knickers… Carry on! What's the sea doing?

PENNY. Filling my knickers?

FRAN. Think poetry!!

PENNY. Er… The wide sea watches my kingdom, er… impassive like the gods…

FRAN. Excellent! Get those impassive gods involved…

PENNY. Oh this is silly, it sounds like I'm doing the washing up with Radio Four on!

JANET. I thought it was going rather well.

PENNY. I just don't feel like it… honestly… I mean the room's not right!

FRAN. We could dress you up! I've got a shield.

FRAN fetches a dustbin lid, hands it to PENNY.

PENNY looks disconsolate.

Well you have to hold it like a proper shield, come on, here… We've got a flag as well, Janet get the flag!

JANET drapes the Union Jack from the piano around PENNY's shoulders.

JANET. And I brought a sword, I thought we might need one, I borrowed it from the Civil War Society.

She hands PENNY a huge broadsword.

PENNY. Bloody hell, Janet!

FRAN. That's it, hold it up in the air…

She cannot, it's too heavy. JANET helps her.

Now how do you feel?

PENNY. I feel like the Britannia on a ten pound note!

FRAN. Precisely, Boadicea, Britannia, it's all the same thing, British womanhood in full armour! Now try again, you're looking at the sea, it's dark, there's a black ship of doom coming.

PENNY. It's a P and O ferry…

FRAN. The sound of the sea…

PENNY. I can't do this, Fran.

FRAN. Janet! The bloody sea!

JANET. Oh sorry…

> *Again* **JANET** *makes the sound of the sea.*

PENNY. We need the lights off… Janet?

> **JANET** *turns out the lights. Suddenly there is a better atmosphere. A pause,* **PENNY** *gets a grip.*

I am a queen now…

FRAN. Use flowery language.

PENNY. I am a flower queen?

FRAN. No! Five words where one would do!

PENNY. Sorry, er… I am Queen… of Mercia… for a moment…'til that ship comes, bringing Roman men. I'm scared of them.

FRAN. Flowery!

PENNY. Er… I fear them… in my… geraniums…

FRAN. Poetic flowers!

PENNY. In my lily-white… soul, and in my… rose-red heart… and know they come to bring my d*oooo*m.

FRAN. Good! Go on.

PENNY. But I fear them not… in my pale woman's… breast.

FRAN. Oh very good! Pale woman's breast, get it all out there.

PENNY. Do you mind if I don't…

FRAN. Why do you fear them?

PENNY. Er… *(building in conviction)* I do not trust them and my fear grows from suspicion, they are violent in their souls, my people are in danger, my unborn children… my unborn…unchildren… *(suddenly a battle cry of sheer frustration)*

> **ANNIE** *appears in silhouette at the door, with a Budgens carrier bag in one hand, the other arm in a sling. She turns on the light.*

ANNIE. Is somebody giving turf?

PENNY. *(swinging the sword to* ANNIE, *barely missing her)* Who goes there?

ANNIE. Bloody hell, who are you?

PENNY. I am Boadicea, Queen of the Iceni and scourge of Rome!

ANNIE. And I'm Annie Taylor, a dumpy housewife from Winkham. You look a right narna up there!

Beat.

FRAN. All right, all right, I think we've lost the moment here…

PENNY. Sorry.

FRAN *notices* ANNIE*'s arm.*

FRAN. Hello Annie, you're late, what happened to your arm?

ANNIE. Fell down the stairs this afternoon, been in A. and E., had to wait for flowers, sorry I'm fate.

JANET. Poor you. Is it broken?

ANNIE. Sprained wrist, daft of me, hair scarpet…

JANET. Stair carpet?

FRAN. These things happen.

ANNIE. They do, they do.

JANET. You're just in time actually, you can join in.

ANNIE. Don't be daft!

FRAN. Did you find anything out about Boadicea?

ANNIE. I've had no time, not with Keith in his condition.

FRAN. What's wrong with him?

ANNIE. He's just a man, he needs constant care and attention.

FRAN. Does he know yet, that you're doing this?

ANNIE. No, I shan't tell him, he'd bill me like a mitten.

FRAN. Sorry…

JANET. Er, 'Kill you like a kitten'? Would he?

FRAN. That seems a bit extreme.

ANNIE. We had two kids, they've gone now.

FRAN. Did he kill them? If so, we should tell someone…

THE BOADICEA OF BRITANNIA STREET

ANNIE. No, but I've been thinking. Like Boadicea, I've lost two kids.

FRAN. You've lost two children?

ANNIE. One to B and Q, the other to British Teleclam.

FRAN. I'm sorry...

ANNIE. He wouldn't have any more, said two were enough, I'd've liked more, mind you, still would actually... I'm not too old, you know, not quite... When they leave the bone you feel so alone... Like an old bra in a drawer – that's a metafact.

JANET. No, that's a simile...

ANNIE. Simile. Right.

Beat.

FRAN. You could try for more... How old are you, Annie?

Beat.

ANNIE. Forty-four.

She starts crying...

FRAN. Are you all right?

PENNY. Well of course she's not all right, look at her, she's forty-four!

ANNIE cries even more.

FRAN. Come on, Annie, forty-four's not the end of the world...

ANNIE. It is! Last time I looked I was dirty.

JANET. Thirty.

ANNIE. - and all my life was still there...

FRAN. It still is, all your life is whatever you've got left at any given point...

ANNIE. Now look... It's not very long is it, fourteen years? But your whole life turns in those years, and nobody tells you they're the best time...

JANET. I'll put the kettle on...

ANNIE. Nobody lets on 'til they're all gone down the lug hole.

FRAN. It only gets worse, love, believe me.

PENNY. Don't say that!

FRAN. *(to PENNY)* You're all right, you're only twelve!

PENNY. Have you got a special diploma in being as hard as nails?

FRAN. I'm not hard, I'm old, your skin grows thick, like wallpaper.

ANNIE. Simile?

FRAN. Simile. *(she hands ANNIE a tea towel)* Here, blow.

> ANNIE *blows. She takes a box of doughnuts out of the Budgens bag.*

ANNIE. Would anybody like a doughnut? I shouldn't I know… *(she takes a huge bite)* I used to be thin, you know, 'til the children, then I just went up like a baboon, and I've been up there ever since…

PENNY. Is that what happens if you have a baby?

ANNIE. It did to me…

FRAN. There may be a valve somewhere we could open?

ANNIE. It's not wind, it's fat!

PENNY. Why do people do it then? If that's what happens?

ANNIE. You'll find out one day. It's lovely, really… I'd do it all again… But it's a shame about Keith, one more would have been nice… Did you have children, Fran?

FRAN. No I never did.

PENNY. Why not?

FRAN. They just never came, you know. I had a job, there were lots of… things… you know.

> *Beat.*

PENNY. Are you going to cry about it? Mrs 'thick as old wallpaper'?

FRAN. No, I'm not going to cry about it!

PENNY. Are you sure?

FRAN. Yes I'm sure! I didn't want any… anyway… That bloody tea ready yet, Janet?

JANET. Brewing! Sorry!

FRAN. What makes you cry then, P.E. teacher? We might as well all have a go.

PENNY. I'm sorry, you were just being so hard to Annie.

FRAN. So were you!

PENNY. I just don't want to be fat!

FRAN. Then don't eat that doughnut! There's an established link between fat and doughnuts you know!

JANET. There's no milk.

PENNY. Great!

ANNIE. Look, this is all a waste of time, we're not getting a thong, we should call it a fright and go zone.

PENNY. What?

Beat.

FRAN. I don't think we should...

PENNY. Why not?

FRAN. I think we're on a high emotional plane, we should use it! I think Annie should be Boadicea, waiting for the Roman men, coming to take her children, her life... and quite possibly her doughnut... Go on, Annie...

PENNY. Oh don't be daft, this is real, not making stories.

FRAN turns the lights out and hands ANNIE the sword and shield. JANET drapes the flag over her shoulders.

FRAN. Go on, Annie, you're in the right place, finish your doughnut and speak.

Pause.

ANNIE. *(chewing, thoughtfully)* If I was her...

Pause.

FRAN. If you were her, come on, say...

Music – underscore beneath the following.

ANNIE. If I was her, I'd like to go back to a time when I was happy...

FRAN. When were you happy?

ANNIE. I was happy with my grandma…

FRAN. Go on…

ANNIE. Going round Winkham market, like a magic place, all these stalls so close together – canvas covers meeting over your head, red stripes, yellow stripes, blue, all these clothes, catching the sun, all these cheap blouses and skirts, and the smell of them, new, crisp, a smell like… babies… that musky smell, all these costumes, like possibilities… I loved it…

FRAN. What was she like, your grandma?

ANNIE. She had this blue coat and blue hat with a wrinkled band around it, she was fantastic, buying wool or curtains, or nets. You remember nets?… Yards of nets… I thought she was the best person in the world, I'd like to go back then, with her, on the cobbles of Winkham market… looking up at her. And if Boadicea had a grandma, I bet she was thinking she'd like to be with her, when those bad men came…

Pause. The music fades.

FRAN. Thank you, Annie. Do you know, you didn't say a single word wrong?

ANNIE. It's the past, I was happy then. I could chalk.

Beat, FRAN *holds her hand.*

'Narration' music grows, then dips to underscore for PENNY *as scene changes.* ANNIE, JANET *and* FRAN *exit.*

PENNY. *(to audience)* And so this weird 'thing' started to get written, and it was nothing to do with Boadicea really, it was all about four women who were trying to make sense of their lives… and I suppose that's what Fran had wanted all along. She was good at getting people together and making things happen… And that's what you need, isn't it?

Music grows.

Another meeting, two weeks later.

ANNIE *appears in the doorway with a huge double bass. The others follow her onstage. During the dialogue they are all handed dustbin lids, wooden swords/broom handles and 'Viking' horned hats by* FRAN.

ANNIE. I haven't played it for years. Keith doesn't like it. It lives in the garage with all my other stuff he won't have in the louse...

FRAN *hands out a page of dialogue, which has been typed up.*

FRAN. I really think we should meet this Keith, he sounds like King Plonker of Plonkton...

JANET. When did you learn, at School?

ANNIE. Yes, and my Grandmother helped, she used to play in a band.

PENNY. Sally Army?

ANNIE. No, Ivy Benson.

PENNY. I'll do the honours. *(She goes to put the kettle on)*

FRAN. Oh, by the way – we've got a date, for our first performance!

JANET. Oh no! When?

FRAN. July 28th.

JANET. We've only got this one page!

FRAN. It doesn't have to be long, fifteen minutes or so, they've got somebody coming from Radio Stoke... they might even broadcast the winner... They wanted a title so I just said what came into my head. *The Boadicea Of Britannia Street.*

JANET. Brilliant! Annie, did you hear that?

FRAN. We can just do what we want, really, bit of drama, odd poem, reflections...

JANET. And we might be on Radio Stoke!

ANNIE. And Keith might die...

PENNY. You mean 'fly', surely?

FRAN. Listen, I want to tell you all something.

Pause. PENNY *comes over.*

PENNY. Well?

ANNIE. Go on, you're making me swervous.

JANET. Nervous, me too...

PENNY. You're going to tell us we're crap aren't you?

ANNIE. She is, she's got that look on her face, like a creature.

JANET. Teacher.

PENNY. What's up?

Pause.

FRAN. I don't care if what we're doing is 'crap' or not – Actually I don't think it is... And I don't care because I haven't had so much fun for a long time – I'm really enjoying myself!

PENNY. Me too!

JANET. And me!

Pause. They both look at ANNIE *expectantly.*

ANNIE. Do I have to say? Only I might cry again...

FRAN. Right! Let's go from the top, this time with the music. Imagine you're addressing your army on the eve of battle, and remember, you're not Annie, you're Queen Boadicea, which means you can speak properly...

They all don their hats. FRAN, JANET *and* PENNY *flank* ANNIE *with the double bass.*

ANNIE. Friends, Romans, countrymen.

FRAN. Leave out the Romans, they're the bastards who are trying to kill you.

ANNIE. Oh, er, friends, Britons, women in arms. I am just a daughter, a mother, and not a king, but I have seen the blood of my country flow...

ANNIE *begins to play – strangled Elgar 'Enigma Variations' – the patriotic sounding bit.* JANET *joins her on the piano, a real dog's dinner...*

PENNY. And though we are weak, and the so-called 'fairer sex', we will stand against our enemies to avenge our fallen.

JANET. And reclaim the free spirit of this ancient land!

ANNIE. There is one Britain, and this is our Britain. It belongs to us all, ginger, blonde, brunette, brown, yellow, red, black or blue!

ANNIE stops playing. **PENNY** *and* **FRAN** *begin to play kazoos – Elgar cont.*

For we are Britons, with the blood of many nations in our veins, it flows like freedom, and if that blood is spilled, if we are oppressed or suffer injustice, then our anger will know no bounds!

FRAN/PENNY/ANNIE/JANET. *(singing – cod opera to the Elgar tune)*
OUR VENGEANCE NO LIMIT!
OUR FURY NO RESTRAINT!

The other three carry on. It is too high, they start screeching.

ANNIE. We will fight like women for our offspring – and we will die like warrior men on the field of battle for our sacred, lost children!

A final flourish of music, as **PENNY** *and* **FRAN** *bring their swords together over* **ANNIE**'s *head,* **PENNY** *having hooked the Union Jack in hers, so it drapes down - like an absurd pseudo classical sculpture. Big finish on piano from* **JANET** *as the Elgar comes to a chaotic climax.*

Pause.

Ooo. Let's have a cup of tea...

Music and blackout.

ACT TWO

Music as all enter.

JANET *is having a cup of tea with* **PENNY** *and* **ANNIE**. *They are waiting for* **FRAN** *at the Institute.* **ANNIE** *offers* **PENNY** *and* **JANET** *a liquorice allsort...*

PENNY. No thanks. You know why...

Pause.

This is weird, she's never been late before

ANNIE. Perhaps she's been run over, or had a strope...

JANET. Well she might just be late, it happens.

ANNIE. Suppose so...

JANET. We could try doing something without her.

ANNIE. Mmmm...

JANET. Well don't sound so enthusiastic!

ANNIE. I'm sorry, I just...

Pause, **JANET** *starts to pick out 'Jerusalem' on the piano. After a while she also accompanies herself on the kazoo.*

Oh God!

JANET. I'm not sure you even like me, do you?

ANNIE. Of course I like you! – I know *she's* got no friends.

PENNY. Ta very much!

ANNIE. Well there was the poem...

PENNY. You shouldn't believe everything you hear.

ANNIE. So you've got lots of friends?

PENNY. No, not exactly... I did have a boyfriend, until quite recently.

ANNIE. So, you're not a vegan?

JANET. Virgin?

46

PENNY. No! I'm the exact opposite of a vegan!

ANNIE. A nymphomoaniac?

Beat.

PENNY. No not a 'nyphomoaniac'. Look, do I make you nervous? Your speech is all to pot again.

ANNIE. Yes you do actually, you both do, very, actually...

PENNY. Why?

ANNIE. Because you're a creature.

JANET. Teacher?

ANNIE. An' you're a... libertarian.

JANET. Librarian?

ANNIE. I never got over that, the creature thing, an' books an' that, and now I've met you pair I'm all... constipated.

PENNY. I'm sorry. Again. Why?

JANET. Yes, why?

ANNIE. Because you're both quite normal, for intelligenitals...

JANET. Oh God...

ANNIE. Like you don't pretend you know everything all the time do you?

PENNY. I do at school, you have to or they'd smell blood, you'd be found scattered along the corridors in meaty chunks like feeding time at Chester Zoo.

Beat.

ANNIE. Can I ask you a question?

PENNY. Yes.

ANNIE. If you're not a nymphomoaniac, what is the opposite of a vegan?

Beat.

PENNY. Pregnant.

ANNIE. Is it?

PENNY. In effect, in my case...

JANET. Really?

PENNY. I'm up the duff, sardine in the tin… bogey up the nostril. A metafact. Preg. Nant.

ANNIE. How did that happen?

PENNY. I do attract the opposite sex, you know, despite being a baked bean, you don't have to get yourself noticed by becoming a barrage baboon!

ANNIE. All right! … When did you find out?

PENNY. About a month ago, about a week before the boyfriend went back to his wife, not that he'd ever actually left her… That's why I came here, to take my mind off it.

JANET. Really? Does Fran know?

PENNY. No. I haven't told her yet, it hasn't really popped up.

ANNIE. Have you told the father?

PENNY. He said he thinks I'm a bunny boiler, and he 'didn't want to face the commitment of becoming a father as he's only just emerging from his own childhood'…

ANNIE. How old is he?

PENNY. Forty-eight, he's head of Maths.

ANNIE. That figures.

PENNY. How?

ANNIE. One plus one making three. You only get that in reproduction, never in baths.

JANET. How come you can say 'reproduction' but not 'maths'?

ANNIE. I have reproduced, I am at ease with the conception. What about his knife?

JANET. Wife?

PENNY. I haven't slept with her…

ANNIE. No, I mean, haven't they got kids?

PENNY. She wouldn't want to lose her figure, she's on the make-up counter at Lewis's, she's got a bottom like two hand-balls, she's waxed, buffed, and shrink-wrapped in nylon.

ANNIE. Fit then?

PENNY. Very.

ANNIE. How did it happen?

PENNY. What do you mean how did it happen?

ANNIE. You know, between you and the head of Baths?

PENNY. Well... You sort've snog for a bit and then the man puts his hand on your...

ANNIE. No! I mean, why did he fancy you if his wife's a wet cream?

JANET. Dream!

PENNY. Being so good-looking she's also got the personality of a Ryvita and shags like a shop dummy, i.e. not really much at all.

ANNIE. Ah... But you fancied him?

PENNY. I do have 'nymphomoaniacical' tendencies. It comes from being an only child and living with my mother.

JANET. Weren't you, you know, using anything?

PENNY. I was using two formica shelves and a plastic chair, amongst other things. Anyway he was in a hurry, he'd got marking to do...

JANET. This was in school!?

PENNY. Maths cupboard.

ANNIE. You're a dark didget. Big cupboard, was it?

PENNY. Big enough for adding up.

ANNIE. Are you keeping it...?

PENNY. I don't know...

ANNIE. When will you decide?

PENNY. Steady on, Annie...

ANNIE. There are loads of people who'd love a baby.

PENNY. I know...

ANNIE. I'm one of them.

PENNY. Fine, I'll just sell it to you then!

ANNIE. That's immortal!

JANET. Immoral!!

ANNIE. It didn't ask to exist, so it seems like adding insult to industry telling it not to.

PENNY. Yes, well, thank you, Annie, there's no doubt which side of the fence you're on, is there?

ANNIE. Sorry, I can't help it...

Pause.

Can I feel your bummy?

PENNY. Tummy! No! Get off!

FRAN comes in. She looks exhausted but is still vigorous, she has a walking stick, the metal NHS sort.

FRAN. Sorry I'm late, had to have a check up. Bastards gave me this... Think I'm old... Still, it was free... Doing some impro?

ANNIE. Penny's pregnant after a casual encounter in a Baths cupboard.

Beat.

FRAN. Oh... *(she gets a chair.)* Did that sort of thing happen in Roman Britain?

JANET. No, she really is, in life not drama, you know...

FRAN. Really?

Beat.

PENNY. Really...

Beat.

FRAN. What a lovely scandal... Whose is it?

PENNY. Mine!

FRAN. No, on the male end of the rogering stick?

ANNIE. The Maths preacher, a married man.

PENNY. Annie!

ANNIE. Well I'm just getting her up to peed!

JANET. Speed!

ANNIE. Penny doesn't know if to keep it or not and he's gone back to his wife because she's got a bottom like two ham rolls and Penny's a runny broiler.

PENNY. I am not a runny broiler! I'm a bunny boiler! I mean I'm not a bunny boiler!! It's the last thing on my mind. I hate children. I have to work with them every day. I can smell a child half a mile away! Why on earth would I want one of the bloody things lurking at home!

A pause. The other three back off.

I've got some wine for my mother in my bag, shall I get it?

FRAN. I think you'd better…

PENNY fetches the wine, and four of the cups. She pours the wine.

I've got vodka, if anyone's interested? We could have a shot of it in the wine?

PENNY. Love some.

FRAN. I thought you were resisting the alco gene?

PENNY. Resisting is not the same as saying no…

ANNIE. You shouldn't drink and be pregnant… you'll lose your licence.

PENNY. Television? Dog? Shot-gun?

ANNIE. Diver's.

JANET. Driver's?

PENNY. Already have, disqualified.

FRAN. Runs in the family then?

PENNY. Yes it runs in the family, like a dripping tap of Budgens own Côtes Du Rhône…

FRAN. Have you broken the news?

PENNY. What, to the father? Yes. That's why he's suddenly found his shop dummy so attractive.

FRAN. No, to your mother.

PENNY. She'll be horrified, she always thought I was a mistake… If she finds out I've done exactly the same thing as her she'll buy shares in Allied Breweries.

FRAN. Have you ever thought you might try being a mother?

PENNY. Not without a dad I haven't. It's one of the reasons I might… you know.

FRAN. I see.

> FRAN *pours the wine, then the vodka in the wine. They all take a big slug.*

Me and Harry couldn't have children. We tried and tried and tried for a while… and that was fun… But this was a long time ago, you know, they can do so much now. Harry always said it must have been his fault, he was such a gentleman like that, he'd always take the blame, but I don't know, we did what we could… Many a night I slept upside down with my legs up the wall to assist the progress of Harry's valiant efforts…

JANET. Too much information!

FRAN. You have to try to imagine me as a young woman, obviously I wouldn't do it now!… Old age is the most infallible form of contraception…

ANNIE. Our two were easy, except Keith was resentable. They were just Johnny failures to him, he wanted to sue Lurex Weathertight.

FRAN. Men can be much moodier than women.

PENNY. I think men have permanent periods, but nowhere for all that anger and pain to get out, unless you count through their little willies…

FRAN. Now you're just being bitter…

ANNIE. That's why they should be bleeded, to let the blood out – you know like bleaches.

FRAN. Leeches. You're as bad as her. You're virtually medieval.

JANET. I don't think I understand men, not really, not like I do women.

FRAN. You think you understand women?

JANET. Well more than men. I mean, I am a woman, so I must understand women a bit...

PENNY. Have you got anyone, Janet?

JANET. No, no one right now, I live with my sister. Mum's still in Manchester. Dad died when I was sixteen.

PENNY. Sorry.

JANET. Thanks... I do miss him, even though he drove me mad. Mum too. I think that's why me and my sister escaped. You have to, don't you, to find out about yourself... no matter if you're a man or a woman...

FRAN. To be honest, I think that people are people and people are different, and it makes no difference if you're male or female.

ANNIE. I don't understand myself, never mind anysoddy else.

JANET. I think I prefer women, on balance.

FRAN. Yes, me too, I think, in the end.

ANNIE. And me.

JANET. No, I mean, I prefer women.

ANNIE. Yes...

Beat.

JANET. No... Big breath... Try again... I've tried both, and I prefer women, to men. I used to think I swung both ways... But I think latterly I've lost the end off my pendulum, so to speak...

ANNIE. *(to FRAN)* She's nymphomanacled an' all!

Beat.

FRAN. Well this is quite a night for revelations!

ANNIE. What's your pendulum? Has everybody got one?

JANET. Some people can't find it.

FRAN. So, you're gay?

JANET. No, I'm definitely not gay, I'm bloody miserable!

ANNIE. *(with great seriousness)* Have you ever actually done it, with a woman?

JANET. Is your next question going to be 'what was it like'?

Beat.

ANNIE. It is, actually, yes.

Beat.

JANET. Well. It was different, it was not so good, it was better… er… it was all of those things…

Beat.

ANNIE. What was the best thing about it?

JANET. Well, I didn't get pregnant like Miss Nymphomanicled over there – lesbianism is nature's own contraception…

PENNY. Well that's great, Janet, the human race can grind to a standstill between your thighs, can't it? Just leave it to the straight girls to do the messy stuff while you have your no-strings fun!

JANET. Sorry, didn't mean to upset you. I can't help it, I just like girls. Er… It's a libraries thing…

FRAN. What on earth do you mean?

JANET. You know, spinsters in woolly tights, Virago Modern Classics!

PENNY. Arrgghhh!! But what am I going to do?

FRAN. Well… I think indecision is nature's way of doing the right thing…

PENNY. I know I could be a mother, but I never thought I'd do it on my own, like my mum did. Or maybe that's the way it's meant to be, and all this nuclear family stuff is rubbish, I don't know…

FRAN. A family is whatever you call a family, and if it's just you and a baby then that's a family… I only had my mum, remember?

PENNY. I'm bound to get post-natal depression, I'm a teacher, I'll probably be psychotic, I'll drink 'til I can't think… and then there's my mother passed out in a puddle of cheap plonk, is that really a family?

ANNIE. Sounds perfectly normal to me, duck...

FRAN. You know, if I'd had the chance of a baby, Penny... This is hard for me... But you must do whatever you think is best, mustn't she, Annie?

ANNIE. Suppose so. Mine are all I've got, even though they've gone...

PENNY. I just don't know how my mother will take it.

JANET. If it's coming down to that, it's silly – having an abortion just because your mother *didn't* have one.

PENNY. Where would I live, though?... I teach – I can't afford a house! And if I have a baby on my own I won't even be able to teach any more, I'll be at the mercy of the DSS!

FRAN. You can move in with me.

PENNY. You don't mean that...

FRAN. Yes, I mean it, I can help you.

Beat.

PENNY. Really? You do, don't you... We're supposed to be writing a play, not this sort of thing.

FRAN. Life is full of drama.

PENNY *bursts into tears.* FRAN *gives her a cuddle.*

I think life is just what passes while you're distracted doing something else, it's like a stupid giant, stumbling by, and if you want to get a grip on it you have to grab him by his giant knackers and pull them so hard that he looks down at you...

ANNIE. Can we put that in *The Boadicea Of Britannia Street?*

FRAN. It's the same story, feeling that your life's not your own, that you're just here for a moment and then it's gone. We're all like the Iceni, standing in a field outside Birmingham in a pair of Janet's woolly tights, wondering how on earth it came to this...

ANNIE. We should be revolting!

PENNY. But luckily we're gorgeous instead!

FRAN. The Winkham rebels! That's what the play can be about... Women of Winkham unite! You have nothing to lose but your—

ANNIE. Husbands!

JANET. Glasses?

PENNY. Jobs!

FRAN. Knickers!

They all laugh, then **FRAN** *starts to cough, cannot stop. The laughter turns into them all watching* **FRAN**.

FRAN. It's all right...all right...

PENNY *brings her a glass of water...*

Thanks... Ugh.

...she gulps the wine instead, at last she stops.

Well, what are you all looking at? I'm not dead yet!

Beat.

PENNY. Are you going to be?

FRAN. Well, not if I can help it, dear.

A pause, **FRAN** *sees that* **PENNY** *has guessed.*

You get more susceptible, that's what they say, it lowers your resistance...the chemo... Well you may as well know... you have to be careful...

Beat.

JANET. Chemo? How often do you have to go?

FRAN. Every few weeks at the moment. I had it before, long time ago, when Harry was alive... Kicked it then.

ANNIE. I'm sorry.

FRAN. A minor problem which I hope to overcome with a vegetarian diet, laughter, and abstinence... *(a glance at the vodka bottle in her hand still)* from cigars...

A silence.

This is exactly why I don't talk about it, people start looking at you as if the grim reaper's outside in a black cab with the meter running...

Beat.

Oh look at you all! Come on! You don't worry about having a heart attack, or falling over and banging your head on a... on a... what are those things in gardens called?

JANET. Lawns?

FRAN. No! No... Hard, little red hats...

ANNIE. Bones?

PENNY. Gnomes?

FRAN. Exactly! We all have to die, and we all have to live! It's a battle – like... like Boadicea! Come on, we've got a deadline. Lets practise the song, come on, the one from the show...

ANNIE. Oh, you don't want that...

FRAN. I do. I really so do...

PENNY. I knew there was something... Look, if we can help at all?

FRAN. *(quite annoyed)* Stop it, please! Look, I wasn't going to tell you, was I? It's a partnership, this illness. Me and my shadow. End of discussion! More to the point, I've got some more words for the song... Will you play it please, dear?

JANET. Yes, yes...

FRAN. We'll record it, so you can learn it... There's not much time – you'll need to learn the words...

She takes out a dictaphone, sets it up.

... Well I'll sing it anyway... This is the new bit... I need you to help me.

The other three snap out of it. JANET *and* PENNY *come to the piano,* ANNIE *gets her bass,* FRAN *and* JANET *work out the chords.*

I'D LIKE TO BE LIKE BOADACEA
RIDING HER CHARIOT, OH WHAT A SCENE
OH TO BE THERE, OH TO HAVE SEEN HER
I'D LIKE TO FIGHT LIKE A WARRIOR QUEEN.

JANET. Shall we try that all together?

FRAN. Yes, let's do the whole thing, from the top! One, two, three, four...

> JANET *starts to vamp,* ANNIE *joins in, with her double bass,* PENNY *sings heartily along with* FRAN.

> IF BOADICEA
> WAS HERE TODAY,
> IF SHE SAW HOW WE LIVED
> WHAT WOULD SHE SAY?

> WOULD SHE PICK UP HER SKIRTS
> HER SWORD AND HER SHIELD,
> CALL TO HER WOMEN
> FROM ANGLIAN FIELDS?

> FRAN *takes the tin (with something rattly in it), which she shakes.*

> (CHORUS)
> I'D LIKE TO BE LIKE BOADICEA
> RIDING HER CHARIOT, OH WHAT A SCREAM,
> OH TO BE THERE, OH TO HAVE SEEN HER,
> I'D LIKE TO FIGHT LIKE THAT WARRIOR QUEEN.

> FRAN *plays the kazoo and shakes the tin, maybe even dances a little, a sense of great joy and abandon as they play the chorus music through again.*

> *Scene change music takes over as* PENNY, JANET *and* ANNIE *re-set.* FRAN *leaves the hall.*

> *A month or so later.*

> ANNIE *wheels herself on in an empty wheelchair. She is wearing sunglasses.*

> PENNY *is making a cup of tea.*

JANET. Have you ever kissed a woman?

ANNIE. What kind of a question's that before we've even 'ad a cup of tea?

JANET. Well, have you?

ANNIE. No!

JANET. Don't you ever wonder what it would be like?

ANNIE. I know what it would be like, it would be like kissing myself.

JANET. Well have you ever done that thing in a mirror, like when you do kiss yourself?

ANNIE. Not since I was twelve, no. To be honest I don't find myself particularly distractive.

JANET. Did you ever, like, before...

ANNIE. Before I got middle-aged and expounded?

JANET. I didn't say that, you said that.

ANNIE. I used to think I was all right, you know, before I met Keith and had the kids, I used to fancy myself a bit, you know – thought I could go out and tug.

JANET. Pull. I think you still could.

ANNIE. Yeah, if I copped off with Stevie Wonder, and then when he grabbed me he'd think he'd got twins...

JANET. I think you're still attractive.

ANNIE. Look, if this is some kind of libraries service chat-up, you can cut it out right now... this lady is not for bending.

JANET. You might like it?

ANNIE. I would not like it! I like blokes, except Keith. It's a tragedy, and it seems to happen to most women... we marry the one bloke in the world we can't stand.

Pause.

JANET. Why are you wearing sunglasses?

ANNIE. I've got very sensible eyes.

JANET. Sensitive. Really? Look, let me help you will you?

ANNIE. What do you mean?

JANET. Ever since I met you that rainy night at the bus stop I've thought...

ANNIE. Thought what? And stop sounding like a Mills and Boon, it makes me swervous.

PENNY *leans forward and gently removes* **ANNIE***'s sunglasses.* **ANNIE** *has a black eye.*

JANET. Thought so...

ANNIE. I walked into a cupboard door.

JANET. Called Keith?

Pause.

ANNIE. He just gets impatient sometimes. He doesn't like to be a bone in the evenings.

JANET. Needs someone to cook his tea for him?

ANNIE. Yes...

JANET. Did he find out you come here?

ANNIE. No, no, he still thinks I'm seeing my lover. My mother! He noticed I'd taken the bass... (*indicating whatever case the bass is in*) 'What the bloody hell are you doin' with the bass?' he says... an' then he says... 'You think you're so special, my lady', he always calls me that, 'my lady', before he does something to me, and then he did this... It didn't blurt though, not this time...

JANET. ...Oh Annie... (JANET *holds her*)

FRAN *comes in, now using her stick, assisted by* PENNY.

FRAN. What's this, forbidden love in Winkham Memorial Institute? You'll be contravening a by-law.

JANET. Fran!

ANNIE. I'm sorry, Fran...

JANET. There's nothing to be sorry about, sorry is an overused word.

ANNIE. You can talk! You say sorry as much as I say sorry.

JANET. Do I? Sorry. Look at her eye.

Pause, FRAN *looks.*

FRAN. Cupboard door...?

ANNIE *shakes her head.*

So that was the arm as well?

PENNY. This Keith?

ANNIE. Yes. I'm sorry.

PENNY. The bastard...

Beat.

FRAN. Nothing to be sorry about.

PENNY. Now you're at it!

ANNIE. No, I mean I'm so sorry because I don't think I'll be able to come anymore, you know, and do the play. If he found out I think he might kill me.

FRAN. He'd have to kill us all, then, wouldn't he?

ANNIE. You don't live with him, Fran. I'm fine when I'm here, but I've got a different knife with him, it's difficult.

FRAN. When did you last make love?

JANET. Fran…

ANNIE. Why?

FRAN. Well he's your husband, isn't he, so when did you last make love?

ANNIE. Sixteen years ago.

FRAN. And when did he last say a kind word?

ANNIE. I can't remember…

FRAN. Did he hit the children?

ANNIE. No, never, he'd not do that, he's not violent, he just hits me.

FRAN. But they left the first chance they got?

ANNIE. Yes…

JANET. So why are you still there?

ANNIE. It's complicated… There's a dog, Moppet.

FRAN. Well if there's a dog I can understand it. Moppet. You'll have to stay then… Give me some of that tea!

JANET. I wonder what Boadicea would do?

PENNY. Oh bugger Boadicea!

FRAN. Well that's not the attitude…

ANNIE. I know what she'd do, she'd put down her sword and give up! Wouldn't you? They'd taken her sand, taken everything…

JANET *softly corrects each wrong word.*

That's how I feel! I feel like I've lost my life and I've just turned into this domestic cave, like a fat lab hat. I might as well not persist... I can't even squeak!

JANET. Speak?

FRAN. Seriously. You can leave him, come stay with me at Britannia Street, with Penny, and Shakespeare.

ANNIE. Who's Shakespeare?

PENNY. Playwright. Big in Stratford.

ANNIE. I'm not Cupid you know!

FRAN. Shakespeare pretends to be a cat, but I think he's a racoon.

ANNIE. We can't both live with you!

FRAN. Why on earth not? Be lovely... Bring Moppet, Shakespeare's always lonely. Janet can come as well if she likes?

JANET. Or you could stay with me and my sister, we've got a little flat, there's a sofa-bed...

FRAN. See! You've even got a choice!

ANNIE. I can't leave him, Fran, he'd kill me...

FRAN. He'd have to kill me as well.

PENNY. We could stop him, you know, like 'stop' him...

FRAN. We could expose him, certainly.

PENNY. Tie him to a lamp post. Tar and feather him...

FRAN. I was thinking this... *(taking a newspaper out)* if you follow my gist...

PENNY. The *Winkham Weekly Snooze!*

FRAN. A more modern take on ritual humiliation. What does he do, Annie? What's his job?

ANNIE. He's an electricution.

FRAN. He's got a respectable business? Customers?

ANNIE. Oh yes... He's even got a little white van.

PENNY. That does not surprise me...

FRAN. So. I do a draft letter about him for the paper, detailing his domestic transgressions, and we deliver it to him first – saying it'll be published if he ever lays a fist on Annie again!

JANET. Perfect!

FRAN. And in the meantime, you'll be safe with us!

Beat.

ANNIE. You'd do that for me?

FRAN. Of course.

ANNIE. Why?

FRAN. You're part of the army, Boadicea's army, on the back foot... We have to stick together!

Beat.

ANNIE. You're a lovely lady, Fran.

PENNY. She is...

FRAN. I'm just doing what Boadicea would do.

ANNIE. Invite everyone to live with her in a Winkham semi?

FRAN. Tell you what, the muse has given us an opportunity for denouement!

ANNIE. Denouwhat?

JANET. The end!

PENNY. What do you have in mind?

FRAN. A battle scene! Boadicea in full charge in her chariot!

JANET. (*pushing Fran's wheelchair*) Leading the Anglian hordes in a suicidal clash – and delivering that letter!

FRAN. All we need is a horse!

JANET. What, a real horse?

FRAN. Well no, not exactly. (*getting up, going to the trunk, opening it...*)

PENNY. What kind of horse is not exactly a real horse?

FRAN. (*she holds the head up high, it is black and white, clearly a cow*) A pantomime horse!

ANNIE. It looks like a cow...

FRAN. Mmm. We need to try it on.

PENNY. She's serious… *(to* ANNIE*)* You'll have to be the arse.

> FRAN *takes out the back of the horse, holds it up.*

ANNIE. I'm not being a cow's arse!

FRAN. It's a horse's arse!

ANNIE. How is that better?

PENNY. You'll have to be!

ANNIE. Why?

PENNY. We'll need something solid to carry Fran!

ANNIE. What?

PENNY. Well I can't, can I? And Fran's the queen, she'll have to ride, and Janet already looks a bit horsey…

JANET. Thanks!

PENNY. So Annie will have to be the cow's arse!

FRAN. Horse! Let's try it for size.

PENNY. What shall I do?

FRAN. You can walk in front with a red flag and carry the letter – Annie – we'll write your Keith a letter he'll never forget!

ANNIE. Great!

> *Music.* ANNIE, JANET *and* FRAN *go behind the clothes rail, or curtains, to put on the horse.*

PENNY. *(to audience)* We wrote the letter that evening so we could deliver it by hand right away… while Keith thought Annie was visiting her mother at the 'hotspot' on the mount… And that's how we all came to be trotting through Winkham… dressed up as a pantomime horse…

ANNIE. *(from behind the clothes rail)* Cow!

PENNY. It's a horse!

> *Impro re: which hole to put your head in, 'does my bum look big in this cow's arse' etc. behind backdrop until all ready.*

> *Music cross-fades with night time traffic.*

The 'horse' trots onto the forestage... **FRAN**, *wearing a joke shop horned Viking helmet and with the sword, mounted aloft (or being pushed by* **JANET** *in wheelchair – but getting her on horse's back is funnier).*

Street lighting, **PENNY** *furtively looks up and down the street with her flag...*

PENNY. Are you entirely sure this is a good idea?

JANET. *(using the horses's mouth)* That's just what I was thinking actually.

FRAN. *(hoisting huge sword aloft)* Completely. When he reads that letter his bubble will burst like a... blown-up Durex at a pin convention.

PENNY. Well I hope so, how's Annie?

ANNIE. *(muffled)* Not really very all right thanks very much!

FRAN. What's the problem?

ANNIE. *(muffled)* What do you think the problem is? Go on, take a wild guess!

FRAN. We're nearly there... come on... HIGH-HO SILVER!!

They travel towards Keith's door.

Blast of a police siren and blue light.

PENNY. *(to audience)* Unfortunately that's when the police car pulled up behind us...

Beat. During the conversation the horse behaves restlessly... **JANET** *also moves its head from* **PENNY** *to the imaginary policeman as if it is listening.*

Yes, officer, this is a pantomime horse...

Beat.

No, we do not have a licence for the public highway... but we do have a red flag, see? *(she waves it.)*

Beat.

FRAN. Who am I? I am obviously Boadicea, Queen of the Iceni!

Beat.

The sword's for self-defence! We're delivering that letter to the husband of this horse's arse.

ANNIE. *(muffled)* I AM NOT A HORSE'S ARSE. I AM A HUMAN BEING!!!

Beat.

FRAN. I had no idea that the word 'arse' was considered offensive, I will not say it again.

ANNIE. *(sticking her head out)* ARSE!

Beat.

PENNY. And nor will the horse's arse!

FRAN. What's he saying Penny? I can't hear, he's only twelve and he speaks like a girl.

JANET. *(using the horse's mouth)* Will you please shut up!

Beat.

PENNY. Ah. Yes, I'm sure Boadicea and her horse would love to accompany you to the station... Shall we just trot alongside?

Beat.

Thank you, Boadicea!!!

Music.

The horse trots off...

Music cuts to reveal:

All four are sitting on a bench at the Police station. JANET *is still wearing the horse's head and front legs,* ANNIE *the rear.* JANET *crosses her legs, panto style, the others do the same.* JANET *neighs in exasperation.*

ANNIE. What are they charging us with?

JANET. *(moving horse's mouth)* Breach of the peace, obscene language, and brandishing a lethal weapon in public.

FRAN. Boadicea never had to cope with this...

PENNY. Boadicea didn't live in Winkham.

FRAN. Will they give me an ASBO? I'd love an ASBO...

JANET. *(taking off the horse head)* Well we could ask them nicely...

ANNIE. It's a judgment on us, we can't deliver the letter, it would be wrong...

FRAN. It's not a judgement. Who's judging?

ANNIE. We're outlaws, desperdoodaas.

FRAN. Read it again... The letter. This is a valuable moment for reflection.

ANNIE takes out a letter from her pocket, unfolds it, clears her throat.

ANNIE. "Dear Keith, I hope you enjoy the letter Fran has written about the local Electricution who beats his wife. It can't be a nice feeling to know that you hit someone who's supposed to be your fiend."

JANET. Friend.

ANNIE. Friend. "If you touch me again, you know what will happen. I'm leaving. I also want a divorce, half the house, and anything else my solicitor asks for."

JANET. *(moving the horse's mouth)* Nice touch.

ANNIE. "Your dinner's in the supermarket, ready-meals aisle."

FRAN. I think it's a work of art, we should put it in *The Boadicea of Britannia Street.*

PENNY. It's going to be a weird performance. I'm not sure what it's about...

FRAN. *(looking up and down the corridor)* It's about being women, and trying to be happy. Come on, they're not looking, let's escape and deliver that letter!

Music, all scarper.

As PENNY speaks a 'Winkham' backdrop is revealed. This could be old panto scenery, or a picture, a draped cloth, or maybe just the SFX and lighting change to imply a hillside.

PENNY. *(to audience)* We heard nothing from Keith, as you might expect, and Annie moved in with Fran and me... Things were getting a bit worse now, with Fran, and so Annie was able to help. I think it made Annie feel better, her mum being in the home and so far gone, it made her feel like she could do something useful for somebody, not just watch the nurses... I was still pregnant of course... I'd done nothing about that.

Music cross-fades with birdsong as the scene is revealed. Maybe, if available, the curtains open to reveal the 'view'.

FRAN *is in her wheelchair.* PENNY *is pushing her up a hill, very steep.*

They admire the view. PENNY *puts the brakes on the wheelchair.*

FRAN. There... Winkham... Like a tapestry... William Morris came here, you know...

PENNY. *(out of breath)* Oh aye?

FRAN. He must have seen all this... It's one of those places that nobody knows but everyone loves as soon as they see it...

PENNY. I like it. I wouldn't live anywhere else, not now.

FRAN. Now?

PENNY. It's such a great place to bring up a kid...

Beat.

FRAN. So, you've decided?

PENNY. Time decided for me, like you said, but I know it's the right thing...

FRAN. I'm glad. Have you told your mum?

PENNY. Yes, she said if it's what I wanted... then fine.

FRAN. So you were a bit wrong about her?

PENNY. A bit. I can't quite see her as a grandma yet though... I left her this morning with a bottle of scotch and forty B and H...

FRAN. Assisted suicide?

PENNY. Well I'd hope it wouldn't stand up in court.

Pause.

FRAN. Can I be a grandma?

PENNY. Fran, of course you can. I'd love that, I'd really love that.

A pause.

FRAN. I love this view, me and Harry would come up here most weekends. Smell the moorland air. It's like taking the roof off your head…

PENNY. It's lovely… Tell me more about Harry, you don't talk about him much.

FRAN. Don't I?

PENNY. No.

Pause.

FRAN. I'll tell you something about Harry. Something that might surprise you…

PENNY. Go on.

FRAN. He's still here…

PENNY. What?

FRAN. He's still here. He's up here with us. *(she takes out the tin she was shaking earlier.)* He's in this tin.

Beat.

Obviously he's dead, of course he's dead! But he came straight back to keep me company… I tease him sometimes. I say, 'Wouldn't you be happier up there you old bugger, with all those angels in the nuddy?' But he just smiles and holds my hand…

Pause.

You think I'm mad don't you?

Beat.

PENNY. I know you're mad, Fran, I don't need to think it anymore.

Beat.

FRAN. There is such a thing as love, you know, it exists. Just like in all the plays and books, and it lasts forever and won't go away, and it makes a bond between two people that nothing can cut... And what you must never lose sight of is that... possibility.

PENNY. I wonder if I'll have that with the baby?

FRAN. The parent thing is not my experience, it seems like a minefield. But you'll love the baby.

PENNY. And if I love the baby?

FRAN. The baby will probably love you...

Pause.

Harry looked after me the first time I was ill. Years ago... He was so frightened he'd lose me. He'd never talk about his heart, he'd this weak heart, a smoker, we all were then. Anyway he started doing exercise and daft things like that, but it was too late... At least this time he doesn't have to worry about losing me... more like worry he's going to get me back...

PENNY. It sounds like he'll want you back, when you do go.

FRAN. I hope so... I'm happy though. I love what we're doing, the play, it's just what I wanted it to be... It'll be a huge hit at the festival I'm sure.

PENNY. Three weeks' time...

FRAN. Three weeks...

Beat.

Just breathe the air up here...

...Harry used to define it, he'd say there are five senses you need to be happy: a sense of beauty, a sense of truth, a sense of right and wrong, a sense of humour, and a sense of what it means to be alive...

You'll be happy. You know that, don't you?

PENNY. I'm so glad I met you, Fran.

FRAN. Don't be daft...

Music.

FRAN *remains in her wheelchair as the scene changes.*

ANNIE *pushes the 'prop' door forward.* PENNY *exits through it, leaving* FRAN *now in her back yard – as at the start of the play.*

ANNIE *comes through* FRAN*'s back door with the pilchard cat snacks and a cup of tea.* FRAN *is clearly now quite ill, still in her wheelchair.*

ANNIE. *(calling softly,* FRAN *wakes nevertheless)* Shakespeare! Shakespeare!

FRAN. *(as at the beginning)* SHAKESPEAAARE!!!

ANNIE. Bloody hell, Fran!

FRAN. Sorry!

ANNIE. Why couldn't you call the bloody cat something sensitive…

FRAN. Such as…?

ANNIE. Flossy, Fluffy, Tigger… That sort of thing

FRAN. Nothing wrong with Shakespeare, great playwright, and a cat lover…

ANNIE. Was he? *(calling)* Shakespeare! *(to Fran)* Does he ever actually come in or is he ferrous?

FRAN. Feral. He comes in now and then, usually dragging a small corpse…

ANNIE. How are you feeling now?

FRAN. Bit better, tablet's doing its stuff.

ANNIE. I've made some tea, cat's lost, no poke.

FRAN. Hope? Joke?

ANNIE. Hope.

FRAN. Love some.

Pause.

ANNIE. What do you think about Janet being a bender?

FRAN. That's a bit of a change of subject.

ANNIE. I was just wondering…

FRAN. I think it's fine, if she wants to be.

ANNIE *absent-mindedly eats one of the cat snacks.*

ANNIE. Do you think I should try it?

FRAN. *(taking the cat snacks from her, handing her back the tea to wash it down)* Well it's not like trying a different cat snack, it has wider consequences...

ANNIE. I know that, but I've failed with my current relationship, haven't I?

FRAN. Well you could try another. Regarding men, there are minor differences if you look really closely.

ANNIE. How do I get another relationship?

FRAN. I don't know, advertise?

ANNIE. What, lonely hearts?

Beat.

Does the *Weekly Snooze* still do lonely hearts?

FRAN. Yes, they call it Men Seeking Women/ Women seeking Men/ er... Men seeking Men or... Women seeking Women.

ANNIE. No animals?

FRAN. That's Pets and Livestock, which is similar but usually doesn't involve sexual intercourse.

ANNIE. Perhaps I should try it.

FRAN. Bestiality?

ANNIE. Writing an ad! You are very bad, you know, for an older person.

FRAN. I just think the unthinkable, my dear. It's the secret of youth, never let the barriers come up in your mind... I could help you, you know, with an ad.

ANNIE. God, would you? I'm useless at that kind of fluff.

FRAN *takes out a pad and pen from her bag.*

FRAN. Right, now, how would you describe yourself?

ANNIE. Middle-aged woman, divorce pending, former victim of domestic violence, overweight, a bit dim, seeks similar...

FRAN. Mmmm. Somehow I don't think that's going to hit the mark, just take what you've written there and change it into something positive.

ANNIE. I can't...

FRAN. You can, look...

ANNIE. Middle-aged woman?

FRAN. Well that could be... 'Lovely lady, prime of life.'

ANNIE. Divorce pending?

FRAN. That's easy, 'newly fancy free'.

ANNIE. Former victim of domestic violets?

FRAN. 'Feisty and with a good sense of humour...'

ANNIE. Overweight...

FRAN. This overweight thing is entirely in your mind.

ANNIE. No, it's entirely on my slips, ties and clips!

FRAN. So we're all supposed to be adolescents with boobs like fried eggs and arms like twiglets? You're a woman, with a woman's shape, you're full-figured, you're Bacchic, you're beautiful, the Winkham Botticelli – you're... 'curvaceous', that's the word!

Beat.

ANNIE. OK, how about 'bit dim?'

FRAN. No such thing. You're 'down-to-earth'... So... 'Lovely lady, prime of life, newly fancy free, feisty, with a good sense of humour, curvaceous and down-to-earth, seeks...'

ANNIE. What do I seek?

FRAN. 'Man', 'Woman', 'Companion', 'Willling quadruped'?

ANNIE. Seeks... 'Like-minded... companion' to share good times with...

FRAN. Optimism is catching...

ANNIE. I feel much better...

FRAN. I'll put the ad in the paper.

ANNIE. You're mad, you know, lovely and mad!

FRAN. That's what Penny said... I hope I am, I'd like to be mad.

Music.

ANNIE *wheels* FRAN *back 'into the house' as the door revolves around them to reveal* JANET *in the institute, putting a small table in the middle of the room.*

ANNIE *enters with a large bag of Cheesy Wotsits between her teeth and a watermelon in each hand.*

JANET. So. You got the melons?

ANNIE. *(dropping the Cheesy Wotsits on the table so she can speak)* I got the melons. Daft idea if you ask me…

JANET. *(taking a melon, uneasily)* The idea, according to Fran, is that we all experience what it might have been like to clout a Roman on the head with a broadsword.

ANNIE. Romans have heads like melons, do they?

JANET. It's the texture, you know, the density, the, the—

ANNIE. The pips and juice spilling out as the brain bursts and the head falls atart… *(she slams the melons down on the table with a thump.)*

JANET. The pips and juice, yes.

Beat. They both look at the melons.

ANNIE. Oh well, got them anyway.

(ANNIE gets her Cheesy Wotsits.)

Fancy a Wheezy Chotsit?

JANET. No thanks. You shouldn't.

ANNIE. Why not?

JANET. Not in your position.

ANNIE. What position is that then?

JANET. Advertising in the paper. 'Curvaceous' will only stretch so far, you know.

ANNIE. Bugger off! I'm a woman at ease with my body. Fran has helped me come to terms with myself as a sexually attractibelle person. There's much more of me in any given clinch than you, babe. You're a slim novella, but I'm a bonkbuster.

JANET. Mmm. Nice description anyway, very creative.

ANNIE. Interested, were you? There's a P.O. box at the *Snooze*. Only thing is, duck, you're still the wrong sex.

JANET. There's no such thing as the wrong sex, there's just sex. Whether it's wrong or not is entirely in the eyes of the beholder.

ANNIE. You don't usually have anyone watching, though, do you? Unless you're a horn star...

JANET. Wouldn't you like to try it?

ANNIE. Try what?

JANET. The wrong sex?

ANNIE. Don't start that again! No, I would not like to try it!

JANET. I read on the Internet that close sexual relationships between women were very common in Boadicea's time, on account of the men being so busy killing Romans, time, and each other...

ANNIE. Yes but that was then and this is Winkham.

JANET. You might like it.

ANNIE. I would not like it!

JANET. Well how will you know if you never try?

ANNIE. I don't want to crow!

JANET. Don't you have a thirst for knowledge? I thought you wanted to write?

ANNIE. How will my writing be improved by kissing a woman? I might be so disturbed I never write another turd, I mean word again!

JANET. Writing is enhanced by experience, Fran said that.

ANNIE. You're not kissing me! I said that!

JANET. Just once?

ANNIE. No!

JANET. You might be the frog to my princess?

ANNIE. I am not your bog! Anyway the bog turned into a prince, not a housewife.

JANET. You might turn into something else.

ANNIE. I will not!

JANET. You might!

ANNIE. Oh God! You're not going to give up, are you?

Beat.

All right then.

Beat.

JANET. Eh?

ANNIE. Go on, then. But no songs!

JANET. Tongues?

ANNIE. No! I mean, yes, you can kiss me if you want to, but no… tongues.

JANET. Really?

ANNIE. Really! What's the matter? Heteroflexibility kicking back in?

JANET. No! … Close your eyes, then.

ANNIE. Why do I have to close my eyes?

JANET. It'll help you forget that I'm a librarian, I mean a woman, well, both!

ANNIE. I doubt it…

JANET. Go on, close your eyes.

ANNIE. You're in denial you know

JANET. What am I denying?

ANNIE. Your heterotestical fate

JANET. I could say the same about you…

ANNIE. That's true…

JANET. So. Close your eyes, pucker up

ANNIE. 'Pucker up'?

JANET. Well whatever it is you do when you kiss someone… God I can't believe I suggested this

ANNIE. Yes, well, I can't believe I'm even pinking about doing this!

JANET. But do you want to?

> **ANNIE** *rolls up her sleeves, wipes away the remains of the Cheesy Wotsits, braces herself on the table, 'puckers up' and closes her eyes…*

With her hands upon the melons **JANET** *leans across the table to kiss* **ANNIE** *on the lips. It seems quite nice – it lasts quite a long time. It ends and they look at each other for a moment...*

JANET. How was that for you?

ANNIE. I'm not yelling you

JANET. What do you mean, you're not telling me?

ANNIE. It was mildly disturbing in all sorts of complex ways and I need to go away and stink about it

JANET. Think. Told you!

ANNIE. Told me what? One kiss doesn't make me a thespian, you know.

JANET. That's what they all say...

ANNIE. What do you mean, 'that's what they all say'? Do you do this all the time? Go round trying to make people glad?

JANET. Gay! No! You're the first woman I've kissed.

ANNIE. But you said you'd slept with a woman?

JANET. Well, in my head I have...

ANNIE. Oh Janet!!

JANET. What? Sorry! I just didn't know what else to do!!

FRAN *bursts in – now with a Zimmer frame, again assisted by* **PENNY**.

FRAN. Look stop arguing you two, we have a problem! He's coming here, I had a call, he's coming here!

JANET. Who is?

FRAN. Keith the Plonker, he's read the ad, he rang me up, wanted to speak to you, Annie, I said you weren't in and wouldn't talk to him if you were and then he was... he was...

ANNIE. Violently obtrusive?

FRAN. I've never heard anything like it!

ANNIE. He can swear like a pooper, it's refartable.

FRAN. Never mind all that! This is serious, we've got about five minutes, what are we going to do?

*As **PENNY** speaks they begin to don a Viking horned helmet each, Fran wears the flag and has the broadsword, they find four dustbin lids and the other swords. It should not be obvious where they are heading with this, though.*

*One melon remains on the table centre stage beneath a dustbin lid. **FRAN** sits behind the table, **ANNIE** and **JANET** stand to her left, **PENNY** to her right.*

PENNY. *(to audience)* And that was how the big event happened really. There were things to hand, you know, swords, and we'd even got some costume together, ready for the big night. I think what I'm trying to say is that it wasn't something we'd thought about, you know, premeditated at all... That's what we said in court anyway...

Back in the scene.

FRAN. He said he didn't care if I printed the article or not, he wouldn't live without you.

ANNIE. Bloody fool, he just needs a cook and a cleaner!

PENNY. But no lover?

ANNIE. Sixteen years is too long for a curvaceous woman to be delicate.

JANET. Celibate.

ANNIE. That's what I said.

FRAN. He thinks he can just walk in here and drag you away like Fred Flinstone.

They are all more or less in position by now.

PENNY. *(to audience)* And it was true, he probably could, except that when he walked in he wasn't expecting to see an old woman dressed as Boadicea brandishing a broadsword... flanked by a pregnant P.E. teacher and a lesbian librarian, all backed up by an East Anglican housewife with a huge bag of Wheezy Chotsits.

They all assume 'battle' positions – suddenly four Celtic warriors.

ALL. Ha!

Music – Celtic, tense. Lights snap to dim and threatening.

A door creaks open, closes with a bang: imaginary Keith.

ANNIE. Go away, Keith, there's nothing for you beer!

PENNY. *(to audience)* He said there was, of course, and that he wasn't prepared to see his own wife advertise for sex in the local paper... Even if she was an idiot.

ANNIE. It wasn't for socks, I just want a fiend!

JANET. Sex. Friend.

PENNY. *(to audience)* Then Fran started up.

FRAN. Not one step more you terrible little man. These women are in my care and I, Boadicea of the Iceni, will not let you harm them!

PENNY. *(to audience)* Which he thought was hilarious, and he came closer.

All but Fran take a half step back.

FRAN. Back! I'm warning you! My blade is sharp as my woman's tongue!!

PENNY. *(to audience)* And he told Francesca Lamb that everyone knew she was dying and what was she going to do? – An old woman in a wheelchair, to stop him taking back his own wife... And that's when Fran stood up.

FRAN. *(standing, heroic)* How dare you! One more step and I will use Boadicea's sword to sever the flesh and break the bones of all our oppressors!

PENNY. *(to audience)* And he told her to stuff it up her jacksy... And so Fran swung the sword round her head twice and...

FRANCESCA *swings the sword around...*

FRAN/ALL. ARRRRGGGGHHHHH!!!!

...and brings it down on the table – severing the watermelon clean in two. The two halves maybe fall off the table...

All four stare at the end of **FRAN**'s *sword, where Keith's head would be.*

PENNY. *(to audience)* And he stood there, with this sword in the top of his 'ead, must have been a good half inch, and then he sort've slowly fell over...

He falls. They watch him go, they all drop their dustbin lids when he hits the ground.

They all look at the imaginary Keith on the floor.

ANNIE. Oh God, Fran, you've killed him!

FRAN. He's a man, they have very thick heads...

ANNIE. We're all going to go to prison! We'll be showering with women 'til we're all wrinkly.

A huge grin appears on **JANET**'s *face.*

It's a preposterous twist of malevolent fate, demonstrating the absolute quintessence of irony... Oh my God, I can talk! I'm cured! It must have been Keith all the time!

FRAN. Is he dead yet?

JANET. Better call an ambulance, I suppose.

FRAN. Better had, yes.

PENNY. *(to audience)* And so the paramedics came and took him away, still with this bloody great sword in his head... and they didn't think it was funny. And the police came of course, and arrested Fran for grievous bodily harm...

An abject tableau: **FRAN** *holds her wrists forward for handcuffs.*

Music.

Later, at the institute, an air of shock. **ANNIE, JANET** *and* **PENNY** *are mopping up blood (melon juice) and wringing it out into a bucket.*

FRAN *comes back in with her Zimmer.*

FRAN. I see you've mopped up the blood?

JANET. There was such a lot, it soaked through, I think it'll stain.

FRAN. Like Shakespeare, his finest tragedies, there's always blood at the end, in buckets.

Pause.

Thanks for the bail...

ANNIE. Don't mention it.

PENNY. The least we can do...

JANET. We went thirds...

PENNY. It was a bargain.

FRAN. Er... How's Keith?

ANNIE. They stiched him up, it seems it missed the brain.

JANET. He'll have a nasty scar, to remind him.

FRAN. Good, good...

ANNIE. They said it was quite deep.

FRAN. The wound? I'm sorry, don't know what came over me.

ANNIE. No, no... the brain, quite deep inside... So the sword... missed it.

Pause.

They all crack up.

FRAN. The police sergeant said, ''Ello 'ello 'ello, you're that Boadicea woman aren't you? Why oh why oh why can't you act your age?'

JANET. Are they charging you?

FRAN. Severe warning. 'In view of the seriousness of the offence' and 'In order to discourage the proliferation of swords in the community.' 'Parently they don't do ASBOs anymore, everybody wanted one...

JANET. Will it be in the paper?

FRAN. It already is, and the article about Keith as well, of course... I gave a statement, they want one from you, Annie, as well.

ANNIE. Will he have to leave the town?

FRAN. They're already talking about an exclusion order…

Pause.

ANNIE. Thank you, Fran, you've risked a lot for me.

FRAN. I've risked nothing. I've nothing to risk, my dear, nothing at all, I'm more excited about how all this will affect next week… We have to get it in perspective, use our experiences. This is a crucial opportunity!

PENNY/JANET. Oh God, next week…

FRAN. Precisely. The performance. Next Friday night at 7.30pm. With all this publicity it's going to be a sell-out!

PENNY. *(to audience)* And so we went into intensive rehearsal. We had various bits that we could put in of course….. and we decided to go with the original title, *The Boadicea Of Britannia Street!*

A final meeting at the Institute. They are putting together a 'running order'.

PENNY. So, there's the song, we should maybe start and finish with that.

ANNIE. And the poems.

PENNY. And the story of me getting pregnant, edited.

ANNIE. And me and Keith, part one.

FRAN. Me and Harry, part one, when he was alive, reflections thereupon.

JANET. Me coming out.

PENNY. Interval…

FRAN. They'll need a break after they realise the Winkham libraries service is in the grip of Lesbia.

ANNIE. Act Two. Sexuality, how to use it, tips for the modern woman.

FRAN. Adventures on horseback, pantomime time…

PENNY. How to decide to have a baby or not, without thinking about it.

ANNIE. Me and Keith, part two.

FRAN. Me and Harry part two, post-mortem.

JANET. Me coming on to Annie.

ANNIE. Censored!

PENNY. The battle of Winkham Memorial Hall, complete with melons!

FRAN. The arrest of Fran Lamb, the 'Winkham Boadicea', as sensationally described in last week's *Winkam Weekly Snooze.*

JANET. It's fab! It'll make them laugh.

ANNIE. Wet themselves.

PENNY. I hope not, they're in those cupped plastic seats – they'll be sitting in it all night...

FRAN. Right. We'll have one more rehearsal tomorrow night, and then it's Friday – and show time!

Music, reflective to underscore.

FRAN *leaves, slowly helped along by* **ANNIE** *and* **JANET.** **PENNY** *watches her go.*

Pause.

PENNY. *(to audience, slightly more formal, as she was at the beginning of the play)* The event was a great occasion, as all of you who attended can remember, I'm sure... And the winner of course was that lovely selection of highlights from *Snow White and the Seven Dwarves* as sung by the Winkham Trio. Well deserved, and nice to hear it on the radio the other night... Our story though, well, our story had a different ending... back at Winkham Memorial Institute the night before.

Music fades.

At the memorial institute, **JANET** *brings in tea for* **ANNIE.** **PENNY** *remains, but she is not in the scene, just observing, as if still narrating the story.*

JANET. Cup of tea?

ANNIE. Lovely.

JANET. I could murder some vodka.

ANNIE. Nerves about the show?

JANET. You're telling me! I'm a librarian, I'm genetically quiet.

ANNIE. Well, if there's anything Fran's taught me, it's face your demons, stare them in the eye...

JANET. Or slice them in two with a broadsword... How is she tonight?

ANNIE. She said she'll be down later after the nurse has been, and we were to start without her... Penny's there, she'll wheel her over... *(she checks her mobile phone.* JANET *notices.)*

JANET. You have a mobile phone now?

ANNIE. I'm a lady at lunch.

JANET. At large. Lady at large...

ANNIE. No, they all ask me out to lunch, I need a phone, to answer all the enquiries...

Beat.

JANET. I'll take you out to lunch, if you like...

Pause.

ANNIE. Will you?

Beat.

JANET. I'd love to, we could start again, from the bus stop, couldn't we?

Beat.

ANNIE. Yes. Yes we could...

ANNIE*'s phone rings.*

I... Yes, all right.

JANET. Well, answer it then...

ANNIE *answers the phone.*

ANNIE. Hello? Oh, hello, Penny...

ANNIE *listens, then takes the phone from her ear, just looks at* JANET.

PENNY. *(to audience, at the podium, a different more formal manner from them all now, in front of their final audience)* It's usual, on these occasions, to say something like, 'Fran lost her long battle'... But it wasn't like that, not with Fran. It didn't matter if she won or lost... This is a memorial service to more than a woman we loved, it's about a way of looking at the world, and at life, that is very precious...

Music, underscore.

...In a funny sort of way I feel that Fran's gift to me was my baby, little Harry, and I know Annie and Janet both feel the same, like they've been given a brand new life...a special second chance... Fran had left a letter... So the next night, while the competition was being held, we all met up again at the Memorial Institute...

Music fades. Next night, at the Memorial Institute, an empty feeling.

JANET. Read it, then.

ANNIE *opens a letter, it has a dictaphone cassette in it.*

ANNIE. *(reading)* 'Dear Annie, Janet and Penny, I'm so sorry about the performance, I really meant to be there. I hope you've had some good times with me, I've certainly had plenty with you, you have made this part of my life easy, and very, very special... and though our journey was brief, it was certainly happy...'

ANNIE *can read no more.* **PENNY** *takes the letter.*

PENNY. 'Look after Shakespeare for me, if he ever turns up. And Janet and Annie, I hope you find what you're looking for – now you both know where to search. Penny, when that baby comes...'

JANET *takes over.*

JANET. '...when that baby comes... choose a name wisely... I'd recommend either Harry, or Francesca. Maybe both?
I love you all very much.'

Pause. **JANET** *looks up from the letter.*

And now she says play the tape, the one we made…

ANNIE. Go on then.

> **JANET** *takes the cassette, puts it in the dictaphone from the top of the piano and presses play.*

> *The recorded dialogue from earlier in the play.*

FRAN'S VOICE. We'll record it, so you can learn it… There's not much time – you'll need to learn the words… Well I'll sing it anyway… This is the new bit… I need you to help me.

> I'D LIKE TO BE LIKE BOADICEA
> RIDING HER CHARIOT,
> OH WHAT A SCENE
> OH TO BE THERE, OH TO HAVE SEEN HER
> I'D LIKE TO FIGHT LIKE A WARRIOR QUEEN.

JANET'S VOICE. Shall we try that all together?

FRAN'S VOICE. Yes let's do the whole thing, from the top!

> **PENNY** *stops the tape. A look to* **ANNIE** *and* **JANET**.

PENNY. She was our Boadicea.

ANNIE. There's still a few of them about.

JANET. Especially down Britannia Street?

> *They share a look, make a determined decision.* **ANNIE** *grabs her double bass,* **JANET** *goes to the piano.* **PENNY** *gets a tambourine. They play and sing the song defiantly, joyfully.*

JANET, ANNIE & PENNY.

> IF BOADICEA
> WAS HERE TODAY
> IF SHE SAW HOW WE LIVED
> WHAT WOULD SHE SAY?

> WOULD SHE PICK UP HER SKIRTS
> HER SWORD AND HER SHIELD
> CALL TO HER WOMEN

FROM ANGLIAN FIELDS?

I'D LIKE TO BE LIKE BOADICEA
RIDING HER CHARIOT, OH WHAT A SCENE
OH TO BE THERE, OH TO HAVE SEEN HER
I'D LIKE TO FIGHT LIKE THAT WARRIOR QUEEN.

ANNIE *twirls her double bass, it spins to a stop.*

Chorus – unaccompanied and in slower three part harmony.

I'D LIKE TO BE LIKE BOADICEA
RIDING HER CHARIOT, OH WHAT A SCENE
OH TO BE THERE, OH TO HAVE SEEN HER
I'D LIKE TO FIGHT LIKE THAT WARRIOR QUEEN.

End of Play

Boadicea

Ade Morris   Paul Kissaun

Boadicea

Ade Morris

Paul Kissaun

Lightning Source UK Ltd.
Milton Keynes UK
UKOW02f0814201114

241898UK00008B/93/P